ONE YEAR
OF WORDS

ONE YEAR OF WORDS

College Vocabulary Enhancement

DOROTHY RUBIN

The College of New Jersey

PEARSON
Longman

New York San Francisco Boston
London Toronto Sydney Tokyo Singapore Madrid
Mexico City Munich Paris Cape Town Hong Kong Montreal

Vice President/Editor-in-Chief: Joseph P. Terry
Senior Acquisitions Editor: Steven Rigolosi
Senior Marketing Manager: Melanie Craig
Senior Supplements Editor: Donna Campion
Media Supplements Editor: Nancy Garcia
Production Manager: Eric Jorgensen
Project Coordination, Text Design, and Electronic Page Makeup: Electronic Publishing
    Services Inc., NYC
Cover Design Manager: Wendy Ann Fredericks
Cover Designer: Maria Ilardi
Manufacturing Buyer: Roy Pickering
Printer and Binder: Courier Corp.-Stoughton
Cover Printer: The Lehigh Press, Inc.

Library of Congress Cataloging-in-Publication Data

Rubin, Dorothy.
    One year of words: college vocabulary enhancement/Dorothy Rubin.—1st ed.
        p. cm.
    ISBN 0-321-12251-8
    1. Vocabulary. I. Title.

PE1449.R817 2003
428.1—dc21

                                                                2003042906

Please visit us at **http://www.ablongman.com/vocabulary**

ISBN 0-321-12251-8

1 2 3 4 5 6 7 8 9 10—CRS—06 05 04 03

PEARSON
Longman

Contents

N.B. Only one definition is given in the answer section. To be sure if an answer is correct, go to the lesson and check the answers with the definitions given in the Answers section.

Preface to Instructors

Vocabulary knowledge is necessary to be able to read and gain concepts. The goal of *One Year of Words: College Vocabulary Enhancement* is to help students acquire a working college vocabulary. The words included here are those that all college students should know to successfully read their college textbooks.

One Year of Words: College Vocabulary Enhancement consists of words that are used frequently in lectures, textbooks, and newspapers. The simple format is structured so it is possible for students to work on their own. To provide immediate results, answers for Practices A and B are given at the end of the book. Teachers can either remove these pages or have students use them to mark their own practices. To ensure mastery of the word meanings and for assessment purposes, a third practice is available for each lesson, and the answers for these practices are in the Instructor's Manual. Two additional quizzes per lesson are also included in the Instructor's Manual.

ORGANIZATION

The book consists of 52 lessons of 10 words each. Each word is followed by its pronunciation, its part of speech, a short definition, and a sentence including it. The

lesson concludes with three practices. The answers for Practices A and B are at the end of the book, but the answers to Practice C are only in the Instructor's Manual. After every three lessons is a multiple-choice test to assess students' cumulative mastery of those word meanings.

SAMPLE VOCABULARY LESSON

- Words are presented with pronunciation, parts of speech, definitions, and in a sentence.

- Practices A, B, and C.

- A multiple-choice test on three lessons is presented to ensure mastery of the words.

Preface to Students

This book has been written to help you become better readers because a good vocabulary and good reading skills go hand in hand, and help make you better students in all the other language arts areas—listening, speaking, writing, and even viewing. It will also help you do better in your classes in all subject areas because when you do not know the meaning of words a teacher uses or those that are in your textbooks, you might have trouble understanding and taking notes in classroom lectures and figuring out assignments.

Even a problem in a content area such as math may stem from a reading problem. Students may be able to do basic math operations, such as addition and subtraction, but aren't able to comprehend the word problems. Also, many of the new math books include more textual explanations than did older math books. And practical mathematical aspects used outside the classroom, such as those involved in cooking, driving, gardening, reading newspapers, shopping, sewing, analyzing reports and bank statements, and paying the mortgage require knowledge of vocabulary meanings.

The more words you have in your listening vocabulary—when you hear the word and you know its meaning—the better should be your ability to be a good speaker, reader, writer, and learner.

The words selected for *One Year of Words: College Vocabulary Enhancement* are words that you will be exposed to in your textbooks, lectures, and in ordinary speech.

Studies presented in the *Encyclopedia of Educational Research* in 1969 suggest that "vocabulary is a key variable in reading comprehension and is a major feature of most tests of academic aptitude." (Walter M. MacGinite, "Language Development," *Encyclopedia of Education Research*, 4th ed. (London: Collier-Macmillan Ltd., 1969), p. 693. Current researchers continue to confirm this and other earlier findings. It is logical that if you do not know the meaning of a word and cannot figure it out from the context of the sentence, you will have difficulty making sense of what you are reading.

Acquiring word meanings is an important language arts skill that should continue through your academic life and beyond. I feel strongly that *One Year of Words: College Vocabulary Enhancement* will help you in this important task.

Lack of word meanings can be painful.

PEANUTS reprinted by permission of United Feature Syndicate, Inc.

ACKNOWLEDGEMENTS

I would like to thank the following instructors for sharing their comments on this manuscript:

Susan Brandt, Volunteer State Community College

Gertrude Coleman, Middlesex County College

Nancy Davies, Miami-Dade Community College

Deborah S. Maness, Wake Technical Community College

Dorothy Reade, North Harris College

Dorothy Rubin
The College of New Jersey
Ewing, NJ

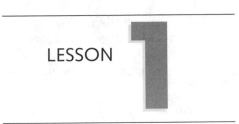

LESSON 1

WORDS

allot	asset	conservative	covet	economize
frugal	liability	liberal	modify	stagnant

1. **allot** (uh • lot′) *v.* To divide or distribute by lot; to distribute or parcel out in proportions; to appoint.
   *Many students confuse the word **allot** with the two words a lot.*

2. **asset** (as′et) *n.* Anything owned that has value; any valuable or desirable thing that serves as an advantage.
   *Most of my friends consider it an **asset** to have a diploma.*

3. **conservative** (kun • sur′ vuh • tiv) *adj.* Tending to maintain established traditions and to resist or oppose any change in these; cautious; moderate; traditional in style or manner; avoiding showiness; one who clings to traditional or long-standing methods, beliefs, and so on.
   *My parents, who don't like things to change, are much more **conservative** than I am.*

4. **covet** (kuv′ ut) *v.* To desire very much what another has; to crave; to long for.
   *My fraternity buddies seem to **covet** many of the women that they see on television.*

5. **economize** (e • kon′ uh • mīz) *v.* To use or manage wisely; to avoid waste or needless spending; to reduce expenses.
   *Because many of my pals spend money so freely, it's obvious that they do not know how to **economize**.*

6. **frugal** (frū′ gul) *adj.* Thrifty; not spending freely; avoiding waste.
   *Even though many of my buddies come from very wealthy families, they have been taught to be **frugal**.*

7. **liability** (lī • uh • bil′ uh • tē) *n.* Something that is owed; a debt; a legal obligation to make good any loss or damage that occurs in a transaction; something that works to a person's disadvantage.
*My wealthy buddies had been taught early on that to owe someone anything was a **liability**.*

8. **liberal** (lib′ uh • rul) *adj.* Giving freely; generous; large or plentiful; tolerant of views differing from one's own; broad-minded; favoring reform or progress. *n.* A person who is open-minded and broad-minded.
*All my buddies at school are **liberals** who favor progress.*

9. **modify** (mod′ uh • fī) *v.* To change slightly or make minor changes in character, form, and so on; to change or alter; to limit or reduce; in grammar, to limit or restrict a meaning.
*The top administrators at our school told us to stop being so destructive at parties and **modify** our behavior or they would take drastic steps to make us change.*

10. **stagnant** (stag′ nunt) *adj.* Lacking motion or current; not flowing or moving; foul, dirty, or bad-smelling from lack of movement; lacking in activity; sluggish; dull.
*There was a **stagnant** pond near our fraternity house that smelled pretty bad.*

Practices

PRACTICE A

Directions: Choose a word from the word list that *best* fills the blank in each sentence.

WORD LIST

allot	asset	conservative	covet	economize
frugal	liability	liberal	modify	stagnant

1. My friend's dorm room always seems to smell like a(n) _____ pond.

2. Many college students often _____ their views later in life.

3. I need to be very _____ with my money because I'm supporting myself.

4. I'm fortunate that I don't have the _____ of a debt at this time because I couldn't afford to pay anything extra.

5. At school, the _____ group was against any changes that were being proposed.

6. The _____ group, on the other hand, was for change.

7. I learned a long time ago that rather than _____ what others have, it was more important for me to appreciate what I could obtain for myself.

8. I have learned to make the most of my _____s and to down-play my faults.

9. She tries hard to _____ because she has lots of school loans and other debts.

10. We try to be as fair as possible, so we _____ equal amounts to everyone.

STOP. *Check answers at the back of the book on page 243.*

PRACTICE B

Directions: Choose a definition from this lesson that *best* fits the *italicized* words.

1. If Jack doesn't start to *economize* now, he will not have enough money to finish the semester. _____

2. Jack's *liberal* views are almost always contrary to his parents' more *conservative* ones. _____; _____

3. Jack says that being at school and on his own has taught him to be more *frugal*. _____

4. Jack was teased about his height when he was young, but now his height is a major *asset*, not a *liability* to him as player on the basketball team. _____; _____

5. Jack says that he has to be very careful about how he *allots* his time. _____

6. Many TV plots are predictable, such as the show on which the handsome cowhand wanders into the ranch house and sees the rancher's beautiful wife; it is obvious that he *covets* her and is going to start trouble. _____

7. Jack said that before his girlfriend visits, he wants to make sure his room doesn't smell like a *stagnant* pond. _____

8. When Jack expects his girlfriend to visit, he *modifies* his studying and practicing schedule. _____

STOP. *Check answers at the back of the book on page 243.*

PRACTICE C

Directions: Define the *italicized* word in each sentence.

1. The *stagnant* water in the pond gave off a terribly foul odor. _____ _____

2. It is smart to begin to *economize* when you are young so that using money wisely becomes a habit. _____

3. Someone who is *frugal* usually knows how to economize and spend money wisely. _____

4. Height is an *asset* to basketball players. _____

5. When my mother went to school, she said she felt that it was a *liability* to be taller than the other children in her class. _____

6. My mother tries to *allot* her delicious pies equally among all of us. _____ _____

7. As a young child, my views were rather *conservative*. _____ _____

8. Later at college, my views became much more *liberal*. _____ _____

9. Even though I know it is wrong to *covet* what others have, there are times I do wish I had their belongings. _____

10. When John was asked to *modify* his loud behavior in class, he tried, but he didn't succeed. _____

LESSON 2

WORDS

adaptation	antecedent	colleague	interrogate	intricate
persevere	precedent	reliable	reluctant	significant

1. **adaptation** (ad • ap • tā ′shun) *n*. The act of fitting or suiting one thing to another; an adjusting to fit new conditions; a modification for a new use.
   Our instructor asked us to read a book that was an ***adaptation*** *of a play.*

2. **antecedent** (an • tuh • sēd′ unt) *adj*. Going before in time; prior; preceding; previous. *n*. The word, phrase, or clause to which a pronoun refers.
   When Melissa writes, she is careful that her pronouns refer to definite ***antecedents***.

3. **colleague** (kol′ ēg) *n*. A fellow worker in the same profession.
   My professor said that she is going to a convention in the summer with many of her ***colleagues.***

4. **interrogate** (in • ter′ uh • gāt) *v*. To ask questions of formally; to examine by questioning.
   When someone in my class was missing money, the police decided to ***interrogate*** *all of us.*

5. **intricate** (in′ tri • kit) *adj*. Complicated; difficult to follow or understand; complex.
   The assignment that my instructor gave the class was so ***intricate*** *that we needed to discuss it at great length to make sure we all understood it.*

6. **persevere** (pur • suh • vēr′) *v*. To persist; to continue doing something in spite of difficulty.
   I intend to ***persevere*** *and finish school no matter what hardships stand in my way.*

5

7. **precedent** (pres′ i • dunt) *n.* Something done or said that may serve as an example; in law, a legal decision serving as an authoritative rule in future similar cases.

   *By working hard and staying in school, I hope that I am setting a good **precedent** for my brothers and sisters to follow.*

8. **reliable** (ri • li′ uh • bul) *adj.* Dependable; trustworthy.
   *My friends are **reliable** people on whom I can depend.*

9. **reluctant** (ri • luk′ tunt) *adj.* Unwilling; opposed.
   *We were all **reluctant** to agree to buy tickets to the game until we knew more about the arrangements and the cost.*

10. **significant** (sig • nif′ uh • kunt) *adj.* Having or expressing meaning; full of meaning; important.
    *We all cheered when we learned that we had done well on a **significant** exam.*

PEANUTS reprinted by permission of United Feature Syndicate, Inc.

Practices

PRACTICE A

Directions: Choose a word from the word list that *best* fills the blank in each sentence.

WORD LIST

adaptation	antecedent	colleague	interrogate	intricate
persevere	precedent	reliable	reluctant	significant

1. My instructors and their _____ attend most of their conferences during the summer.

2. As there were no _____ to follow, our instructors decided to make up their own.

3. We said we would vote for Pat for school council because we felt she was the most _____ candidate.

4. Pat said that she would _____ regardless of the odds against her winning.

5. Pat doesn't like to be questioned, so she particularly didn't like being _____ by the other students.

6. Pat said that she was _____ to run for office because she didn't like to campaign for votes.

7. We told Pat that it was _____ that so many people wanted her to be elected.

8. Pat soon learned about the _____ details involved in running for office.

9. When Pat spoke, she made sure that she used pronouns that referred to a definite _____.

10. We tried to get Pat to relax before the election by taking her to see a movie that was a(n) _____ of a book we had all read.

> **STOP.** *Check answers at the back of the book on page 243.*

PRACTICE B

Directions: Choose a definition from this lesson that *best* fits the *italicized* words.

1. The judge's decision will serve as a *precedent* for future cases. _____

2. The event was *antecedent* to the war and may have been the cause of it. _____

3. Only *reliable* people were chosen for the mission because they had to be trusted with secret information. _____

4. Many people were *reluctant* to run for office at our school. _____

5. The results of the meeting were so *significant* that it will change the way things are done in the future. _____

6. My professor said he was meeting several of his *colleagues* at the convention. _____

7. We concluded that some methods used to *interrogate* people are cruel and inhumane. _____

8. The *intricate* dress pattern was so complicated that I asked someone to help me with it. _____

9. That new television show, which is an *adaptation* of an older one, is well suited for today's audience. _____

10. Some people tend to give up rather than *persevere* when things get difficult. _____

> **STOP.** *Check answers at the back of the book on page 243.*

PRACTICE C

Directions: Define the *italicized* word in each sentence.

1. The play is an *adaptation* of a well-known book. _____ _____

2. The detectives decided to *interrogate* all those present at the crime scene. _____

3. The *antecedent* of <u>he</u> in the sentence "Carlos is a handsome man, and he seems to know this" is <u>Carlos</u>. _____

4. Shawna and her *colleague* from school went to the science conference together. _____

5. Please teach me the song with the *intricate* harmonies. _____ _____

6. Melissa said that she was *reluctant* to go to the fraternity party. _____ _____

7. Melissa said that she learned from a *reliable* source that it was going to be a very wild party. _____

8. Jason told Melissa that the calm parties this fraternity had given before set the *precedent* for this also being a quiet event._____

9. Regardless of what Jack said, Melissa was determined to *persevere* and not go. _____

10. It is *significant* that the party was as quiet as the others the fraternity had given and was not the wild event Melissa had been warned about. _____ _____

LESSON 3

WORDS

affirm	coincidence	delete	dilemma	diligent
disdain	eradicate	haughty	isolate	pertinent

1. **affirm** (uh • firm') *v.* To declare or state positively; to declare or state that something is true.

   *Our treasurer went over our sorority's account books and she **affirmed** that our finances were in order.*

2. **coincidence** (kō • in' suh • dens) *n.* The occurrence of things or events at the same time by chance.

   *It was quite a **coincidence** to find him in Paris at the same time that I was there.*

3. **delete** (di • lēt') *v.* To take out or remove a letter, word, or other element; to cross out; to erase.

   *I like writing on my computer because I can **delete** any word or paragraph easily.*

4. **dilemma** (duh • lem' uh) *n.* Any situation that necessitates a choice between equally unfavorable or equally unpleasant alternatives; an argument that presents two equally unfavorable alternatives.

   *I'm facing a **dilemma**, because I do not want to do my homework or go to the language lab.*

5. **diligent** (dil' uh • jent) *adj.* Applying oneself in whatever is undertaken; working in a constant effort to accomplish something; industrious.

   *At school we've noticed that the **diligent** students are the ones who get the best grades.*

6. **disdain** (dis • dān') *v.* To regard as unworthy; to despise. *n.* The feeling of scorn or contempt; expression of scorn.

   *When people learned that I was giving test answers to other students, they looked upon me with **disdain**.*

7. **eradicate** (uh • rad′ uh • kāt) *v.* To destroy completely; to pull out by the roots; to wipe out; to exterminate.
   *The engineering students had to **eradicate** any errors from their model before they could start to build the actual machine.*

8. **haughty** (haw′tē) *adj.* Having or showing great pride in oneself and contempt, disrespect, or scorn for others; overbearing; snobbish; arrogant.
   *The manner of the rich boy was so **haughty** that no one wanted to be around him.*

9. **isolate** (ī′suh • lāt) *v.* To set apart from others; to place alone; to separate.
   *When Peter was caught driving without a license, the police brought him to the police station and put him in a room to **isolate** him from other prisoners.*

10. **pertinent** (pur′ tuh • nunt) *adj.* Relevant; relating to or bearing on the matter in hand; being to the point.
    *At the police station, my friend said he had **pertinent** information concerning why Peter was driving without his license.*

PEANUTS reprinted by permission of United Feature Syndicate, Inc.

Practices

PRACTICE A

Directions: Choose a word from the word list that *best* fits the blank in each sentence.

WORD LIST

affirm	coincidence	delete	dilemma	diligent
disdain	eradicate	haughty	isolate	pertinent

1. We thought that it was quite a(n) _____ that the twins sitting in different parts of the room got the same answers on the exam wrong.

2. Sara knew that she faced a terrible _____ because whatever choice she made would have an unpleasant effect on others.

3. We were told by our instructor to only insert _____ information that was related to the topic.

4. Peter said that his witnesses would _____ that he does have a license.

5. Peter's lawyer told Peter that his _____ and unpleasant manner offended the police and would not help his case.

6. Peter explained that he didn't mean to behave that way, but he did not like it when the police treated him as if he had a contagious disease and needed to _____ him.

7. Peter hoped to be able to _____ this little adventure from his permanent record.

8. The police officer told Peter that if he paid a fine, he would _____ Peter's name from the list.

9. In spite of his contrite words, Peter still looked with _____ at the police for taking him to the station.

10. Peter should be as _____ about taking his driver's license test as he is about apologizing for being caught driving without one.

> **STOP.** *Check answers at the back of the book on page 243.*

PRACTICE B

Directions: Choose a word from this lesson that *best* matches the meaning of the *italicized* words.

1. People usually dislike an *overbearing* person. _____

2. We were told that the school intended to *tear down* our old dorm. _____

3. It was quite *by chance* that Sharon and I were trying to call each other at the same time, causing us each to get busy signals. _____

4. We told Aretha that to avoid being a wallflower at parties, she should not *set herself apart* from the others. _____

5. The lawyer said that he wanted to *state positively* that his client was innocent. _____

6. & 7. Seth said that he wouldn't *take out* one word from his report because all the words were *relevant.* _____; _____

8. Peter's friends told him that if he continues to behave in the same way, others would look upon him with *scorn*. _____

9. Mary is such a success because she is an *industrious* worker. _____

10. When we found ourselves facing *a situation* in which we had to choose between an equally bad set of alternatives, we didn't know what to do. _____

> **STOP.** *Check answers at the back of the book on page 243.*

PRACTICE C

Directions: Define the *italicized* word in each sentence.

1. Kelsey looked with *disdain* on those who cheated on the exam. _____ _____

2. My *dilemma* is worrisome because if I choose to have the transplant, I may die, but if I don't, I also might die._____

3. If I were you, I would not *delete* one word from the story because it is excellent as it is. _____

4. I dislike *haughty* people because they are so overbearing. _____ _____

5. He wanted to *eradicate* the arrest from his record. _____ _____

6. I know it's a *coincidence*, but it's so weird that almost every time the phone rings, my doorbell also rings. _____

7. My instructor *affirmed* to us that she would finish grading our finals by tomorrow. _____

8. José is a *diligent* young man who excels at whatever task he undertakes. _____

9. It's *pertinent* to your getting better that you follow the doctor's advice carefully. _____

10. We told Erin that if she continues to *isolate* herself from others, she will not have many friends. _____

Multiple-Choice Assessment of Lessons 1–3

Directions: Words are arranged by lesson. Underline the meaning that *best* fits the word. Answers are at the back of the book. **If you miss any word meaning, go back to the lesson and restudy the word.**

LESSON 1

1. **allot**
   a. to donate
   b. to state an opinion
   c. to tell a lot
   d. to divide

2. **asset**
   a. to assess
   b. happy
   c. a valuable thing
   d. an opinion

3. **conservative**
   a. tending to like change
   b. tending to like differences
   c. tending to be broad-minded
   d. tending to like things to remain the same

4. **covet**
   a. to like things
   b. to dislike things
   c to desire things that others have
   d. to hope

5. **economize**
   a. to spend freely
   b. to spend money
   c. refers to economics
   d. to avoid waste

6. **frugal**
   a. spends freely
   b. wise
   c. spends often
   d. thrifty

7. **liability**
   a. a gift
   b. legal
   c. a debt
   d. a feeling

8. **liberal**
   a. big
   b. broad-minded
   c. remain the same
   d. helpful

9. **modify**
   a. to change slightly
   b. to move
   c. to dress
   d. to be mod

10. **stagnant**
    a. lacking movement
    b. moving
    c. healthful
    d. refers to running water

LESSON 2

11. **adaptation**
    a. act of adjusting to old situations
    b. a fitting outcome
    c. refers to adoption
    d. act of fitting one thing to another

12. **antecedent**
    a. going against
    b going after
    c. going before
    d. going first

13. colleague
a. a college buddy
b. a friend
c. an enemy
d. a fellow worker in a profession

14. interrogate
a. to speak
b. to state
c. to question
d. to make a choice

15. intricate
a. complicated
b. simple
c. presenting a problem
d. helpful

16. persevere
a. to help
b. to persist
c. to move
d. to be active

17. precedent
a. something that serves as an example
b. an offense
c. something unnecessary
d. something that comes after

18. reliable
a. helpful
b. dependable
c. hostile
d. presenting an example

19. reluctant
a. willing
b. helping
c. unwilling
d. hostile

20. significant
a. a sign
b. a meaning
c. helpful
d. important

LESSON 3

21. affirm
a. to deny
b. to ask
c. to question
d. to state positively

22. coincidence
a. something that happens
b. a chance
c. occurrence of things at the same time by chance
d. a happening

23. delete
a. to put in
b. to take out
c. to write
d. to allow

24. dilemma
a. a problem
b. an argument
c. something unpleasant
d. a choice usually between two equally disagreeable things

25. diligent
a. a choice
b. a choice between disagreeable things
c. applying oneself
d. an argument

26. disdain
a. a disagreement
b. a chance happening
c. to regard as unworthy
d. to apply oneself

27. eradicate
  a. to despise
  b to disagree
  c. to wipe out completely
  d. to change

28. haughty
  a. having good self-esteem
  b. arrogant
  c. disagreeable
  d. hostile

29. isolate
  a. to harm
  b. to help
  c. to set apart
  d. to stay together

30. pertinent
  a. unrelated
  b. not appropriate
  c. appropriate
  d. set apart

STOP. *Check answers at the back of the book on page 243.*

LESSON 4

candid	frustrate	inquisitive	integrate	naïve
segregate	sustain	tacit	terse	verbose

1. **candid** (kan′ did) *adj.* Honest, outspoken; frank.
   *You know that Joshua is **candid** about his views because he always says what he thinks.*

2. **frustrate** (frus′ trāt) *v.* To defeat; to bring to nothing. *adj.* Frustrated; filled with a sense of discouragement and dissatisfaction as a result of defeated efforts, inner conflicts, or unsolved problems.
   *They were unable to **frustrate** my friend Joshua in his bid for school office.*

3. **inquisitive** (in • kwiz′ uh • tiv) *adj.* Curious; asking many questions; improperly or unnecessarily curious; prying.
   *My **inquisitive** roommate kept asking me questions about Joshua's date with the homecoming queen.*

4. **integrate** (in′ tuh • grāt) *v.* To unite; to make whole or complete by adding together parts.
   *I feel that my roommate is trying to discredit Joshua so that he can **integrate** certain student groups into a bloc to vote for his candidate.*

5. **naïve** (nī • ēv′) *adj.* Foolishly simple; unsophisticated; childlike.
   *My roommate must think that I am pretty **naïve** to fall for his attempts to pump me for information about Joshua.*

6. **segregate** (seg′ ruh • gāt) *v.* To set apart from others; to separate.
   *Joshua is against those who **segregate** themselves from other students by forming clubs that do not offer membership to all.*

7. **sustain** (sus • tān′) *v.* To maintain; to keep in existence; to keep going; to uphold.
   *I tried hard to **sustain** and support Joshua when the going got rough during his campaign.*

8. tacit (tas' it) *adj.* Unspoken; not expressed openly.

*Joshua and I have a **tacit** agreement about many things, so we often do not need to say much to one another.*

9. terse (turs) *adj.* Brief; concise.

*Joshua always gives **terse** speeches because he knows that the students do not like long ones.*

10. verbose (vur • bōs') *adj.* Wordy.

*Fortunately for Joshua, those running against him made such **verbose** speeches that the students became restless.*

SHOE reprinted by permission of Tribune Media Services.

Practices

PRACTICE A

Directions: Choose a word from the word list that *best* fits the blank in each sentence.

WORD LIST

candid	frustrate	inquisitive	integrate	naïve
segregate	sustain	tacit	terse	verbose

1. Peter tends to _____ himself from others because he is a loner.

2. My _____ friend Bethany went to Jake's apartment to see his etchings, but he had other things on his mind.

3. There are times that it pays to be _____; however, there are also times when being outspoken can cause you grief.

4. The _____ reporters continued to pry into the affairs of the politician until they arrived at the truth.

5. Many people tried to _____ the reporters' attempts at discovering the truth.

6. In the film, the students had a _____ agreement to bang their desks every time the teacher turned her back.

7. Erin's answers are always _____ and to the point.

8. In contrast, Eram's answers are never short; they are _____.

9. Several companies have merged and as a result have tried to _____ their staffs into a new operation.

10. Since my friend's parents have both been laid off from their jobs, they are finding it hard to _____ their former standard of living.

> **STOP.** *Check answers at the back of the book on page 243.*

PRACTICE B

Directions: Choose a word from this lesson that *best* matches the meaning of the *italicized* word.

1. José found out the hard way that it is difficult to *maintain* oneself on a meager diet while working and going to school. _____

2. The *unsophisticated* candidate appeared childlike next to the worldly diplomat. _____

3. I do not like to attend one of my classes because the instructor seems to do everything in his power to *defeat* my desire to learn. _____

4. The police said that the *prying* reporter had been murdered by the mobsters because he had uncovered information that the mobsters wanted concealed. _____

5. Stella was pretty *outspoken* when she told the instructor that her lectures were over most of the students' heads. _____

6. There seems to be an *unspoken* agreement among the students that no one ask a question toward the end of class period. _____

7. One of my instructors is so *wordy* that it takes her about five minutes to say "Hi." _____

8. We were told that there is a plan in the works to *unite* two of our departments into one new one. _____

9. The students told the candidates to make *brief* statements because it was close to noon. _____

10. Public clubs today aren't supposed to *separate* some people from others. _____

> **STOP.** *Check answers at the back of the book on page 243.*

PRACTICE C

Directions: Match the number of the word in Column A with the letter of its meaning in Column B.

	Column A	*Column B*
_____	1. candid	a. curious
_____	2. frustrate	b. to maintain
_____	3. tacit	c. brief
_____	4. segregate	d. childlike
_____	5. inquisitive	e. unspoken
_____	6. terse	f. wordy
_____	7. verbose	g. to unite
_____	8. sustain	h. to separate
_____	9. naïve	i. honest
_____	10. integrate	j. to defeat

WORDS

affluent	alternative	concise	famish	fatigue
formidable	mundane	nostalgic	optimist	pessimist

1. **affluent** (af′ lū • ent) *adj.* Wealthy; having an abundance of goods or riches.
   *Although Alfredo is quite **affluent**, you would never know he is wealthy from the way he acts.*

2. **alternative** (awl • tur′ nuh • tiv) *n.* One or more things offered for choice; a choice between two or more things; a remaining choice; a choice. *adj.* Offering or providing a choice between two or more things.
   *It was a no-brainer that I would choose the third **alternative** and go to the concert rather than stay at home on a Saturday night.*

3. **concise** (kun • sīs′) *adj.* Brief; terse.
   *Jim's instructor said that the students' reports should be **concise** and to the point.*

4. **famish** (fam′ ish) *v.* To make or be very hungry; starve. *adj.* (famished) Very hungry.
   *After gym period, we were so **famished** that we felt we could eat almost anything.*

5. **fatigue** (fuh • tēg′) *n.* Physical or mental tiredness; weariness. *v.* To tire out; to weary; to weaken from continued use.
   *After I finished writing my psychology paper, I was so **fatigued** that I felt I could sleep for a week.*

6. **formidable** (for′ mid • uh • bul) *adj.* Dreaded; causing awe or fear; hard to handle; of discouraging or awesome strength, size, difficulty, and so on.
   *I thought that the psychology assignment was such a **formidable** one that I put off starting it.*

7. mundane (mun' dān) *adj.* Referring to everyday things; referring to that which is routine or ordinary; referring to worldly things rather than more high-minded or spiritual things.

*While I was trying to finish my psychology assignment, I neglected all the **mundane** things that I normally do, such as washing clothes, sleeping a decent number of hours, and eating properly.*

8. nostalgic (nuh • stal'jik) *adj.* Homesick; longing to go back to one's home, hometown, and so on; longing for something far away or long ago.

*While working on my psychology assignment, I became very **nostalgic** for my high school days, when my mother took care of all my needs.*

9. optimist (op' tuh • mist) *n.* One who is hopeful; a cheerful person; one who takes the most hopeful view or expects the best outcome.

*Because I am an **optimist**, I expect to get a great grade on my psychology paper.*

10. pessimist (pes' uh • mist) *n.* One who expects the worst to happen in any situation; a gloomy person; one who looks on the dark side of things.

*My roommate is a **pessimist**; therefore, he always expects to get crummy grades on his papers, even when he works hard on them.*

Practices

PRACTICE A

Directions: Choose a word from the word list that *best* fits the blank in each sentence.

WORD LIST

affluent	alternative	concise	famish	fatigue
formidable	mundane	nostalgic	optimist	pessimist

1. When Jack's mother phoned for him to come home immediately because of a family crisis, Jack felt that he had no _____ but to go home.

2. Even though Jack's parents weren't _____, they did provide for him and his sister and sent them to the schools of their choice.

3. Jack is known at school as a(n) _____, because he's always looking at the cheerful side of things, but he was concerned after he heard his mother's voice.

4. Jack was so _____ from taking midterms that before his mother's call, he was looking forward to sleeping for at least a week.

5. However, Jack isn't a(n) _____, and although he was worried by the phone call, he felt that there were some good things about going home.

6. Jack's mother is a good cook, and because he was _____ from skipping meals while he was studying, he was looking forward to eating her dinners again.

7. As Jack drove home, he became more and more _____; he didn't realize how much he had missed seeing everyone and hanging out in his old haunts.

8. Someone once said that it's the everyday, _____ things that you take for granted and really miss when you don't have them anymore.

9. The trip home was a(n) _____ one because Jack was driving by himself, and he lived quite a distance from his college campus.

10. Jack was _____ and gave few details when he told us he had to hurry home.

> **STOP.** *Check answers at the back of the book on page 243.*

PRACTICE B

Directions: Choose a word from the word list that *best* matches the meaning of the *italicized* word(s).

WORD LIST

affluent	alternative	concise	famish	fatigue
formidable	mundane	nostalgic	optimist	pessimist

1. I become *homesick* for my familiar surroundings and friends after being away for a long time. _____

2. After studying for all my exams, I was so *mentally and physically tired* that I collapsed. _____

3. Writing three papers in one week is *hard to handle*. _____

4. When I study for exams, I often don't eat, so I feel *starved* when they are over.
   _____

5. Sharon is a *person who always looks on the bright side of things*.
   _____

6. Her brother Eram, on the other hand, is a *person who always looks on the dark side of things.* _____

7. Writing papers and taking exams is a *routine or ordinary* part of life for most students. _____

8. Jack felt that he had no *choice* in the matter, so he went home. _____ _____

9. In school I learned that it's best to answer questions in a *brief* way. _____

10. Most of my friends come from *wealthy* homes, but they don't behave like snotty kids who are used to getting everything they want. _____

STOP. *Check answers at the back of the book on page 243.*

PRACTICE C

Directions: Match the number of the word in Column A with the letter of its meaning in Column B.

	Column A	*Column B*
_____	1. affluent	a. starve
_____	2. alternative	b. brief
_____	3. pessimist	c. one who is hopeful
_____	4. fatigue	d. homesick
_____	5. mundane	e. commonplace
_____	6. formidable	f. one who expects misfortune
_____	7. optimist	g. dreaded
_____	8. concise	h. a choice
_____	9. famish	i. wealthy
_____	10. nostalgic	j. weariness

LESSON 6

WORDS

amnesty	covert	curtail	fatal	fictitious
hostile	lethal	overt	relevant	sentimental

1. **amnesty** (am′ nes • tē) *n*. A pardon from the government; the act of letting someone off.
   *Cindy received a pardon after all because the government changed its policy on the granting of **amnesty**.*

2. **covert** (kō′ vurt) *adj*. Secret; concealed; covered over; sheltered.
   *They behaved in such a **covert** manner that everyone at school knew they were trying to hide something.*

3. **curtail** (kur tāl′) *v*. To shorten; to lessen; to cut off the end or a part.
   *After Pat lost his job, he is buying fewer clothes and eating out less to **curtail** expenses.*

4. **fatal** (fā′ tul) *adj*. Resulting in or capable of causing death; deadly; bringing ruin or disaster; having decisive importance.
   *After Selina had a **fatal** accident in her friend's car, the whole school attended a memorial for her.*

5. **fictitious** (fik • ti′ shus) *adj*. Imaginary; not real; made up; fabricated.
   *The information on the Internet about me was **fictitious** with no basis in fact.*

6. **hostile** (hos′ tīl) *adj*. Unfriendly; referring to an enemy.
   *My former best friend is so **hostile** to me that he is spreading vicious, untrue tales about me on the Internet.*

7. **lethal** (lē′ thul) *adj*. Causing death; deadly.
   *Actually, I was so disgusted with my former best friend that I wanted to give him a **lethal** dose of something.*

8. **overt** (ō′ vurt) *adj.* Open to view; public; apparent; able to be seen.
*My former best friend doesn't hide his dislike for me; he is quite **overt** about it.*

9. **relevant** (rel′ uh • vunt) *adj.* Applying to the matter in question; suitable; relating to; pertinent.
*What my former best friend says about me on the Internet isn't **relevant** to anything that we ever discussed or talked about.*

10. **sentimental** (sen • tuh • men′ tul) *adj.* Marked by tenderness, emotion, feeling, and so on; influenced more by feeling or emotion than by reason; acting from feeling rather than from practical motives.
*I became so **sentimental** toward my home after I had been away for awhile that I couldn't wait to return, even though just a few months ago, I couldn't wait to leave.*

Practices

PRACTICE A

Directions: Choose a word from the word list that *best* fits the blank in each sentence.

WORD LIST

amnesty	covert	curtail	fatal	fictitious
hostile	lethal	overt	relevant	sentimental

1. To hide his identity, Karl used a(n) _____ name when he went in chat rooms on the Internet.

2. He did so to help the police track down the person who had met his friend Donna in a chat room and then killed her with a(n) _____ dose of poison.

3. Karl still couldn't believe that Donna had died from a(n) _____ dose of poison.

4. To help catch the killer, Karl infiltrated the chat room and behaved in a(n) _____ manner.

5. Because Karl wanted to help find Donna's murderer, he started participating in the streams of conversation in the chat room and tried not to react in a way that was _____ or angry.

6. The problem that Karl had with his undercover work was that he did not know whether what someone said to him in the chat room was _____ to the investigation or if a statement was unconnected to it.

7. The police told Karl to make sure he noted the name and meeting place of anyone who wanted to see him but to be brief and _____ the discussions with the person.

8. The police told Karl that they were willing to give _____ to an informant who knew something about Donna's death as long as he told on others who were preying on young women.

9. The police thought that Karl was perfect to help them because he had a(n) _____ manner and didn't seem to be hiding anything.

10. Karl was also a(n) _____ person who felt very emotional about Donna's murder, so the police thought that he would appeal to the person who had lured her to her death.

> **STOP.** Check answers at the back of the book on page 243.

PRACTICE B

Directions: Match the meaning with the word from the word list.

WORD LIST

amnesty	covert	curtail	fatal	fictitious
hostile	lethal	overt	relevant	sentimental

1. Secret _____

2. Deadly _____

3. A pardon from the government _____

4. Open to view _____

5. To shorten _____

6. Suitable _____

7. Unfriendly _____

8. Imaginary _____

9. Marked by tenderness _____

10. Causing death _____

> **STOP.** *Check answers at the back of the book on page 243.*

PRACTICE C

Directions: Match the number of the word in Column A with the letter of its meaning in Column B.

	Column A	*Column B*
_____	1. amnesty	a. deadly
_____	2. curtail	b. unfriendly
_____	3. relevant	c. able to be seen
_____	4. fatal	d. marked by emotion
_____	5. overt	e. causing death
_____	6. fictitious	f. secret
_____	7. hostile	g. imaginary
_____	8. covert	h. to shorten
_____	9. lethal	i. a pardon from the government
_____	10. sentimental	j. suitable

Multiple-Choice Assessment of Lessons 4–6

Directions: Words are arranged by lesson. Underline the meaning that *best* fits the word. Answers are at the end of the book. **If you miss any word meaning, go back to the lesson and restudy the word.**

LESSON 4

1. candid
a. happy
b. cheerful
c. frank
d. to the point

2. frustrate
a. to defeat
b. to separate
c. anxious
d. foolish

3. inquisitive
   a. prying
   b. wise
   c. a quiz
   d. going before

4. integrate
   a. to separate
   b. to unite
   c. to untie
   d. race

5. naïve
   a. happy
   b. childlike
   c. sophisticated
   d. apathetic

6. segregate
   a. to unite
   b. foolish
   c. regulate
   d. to separate

7. sustain
   a. to help
   b. unnecessary
   c. to maintain
   d. to go

8. tacit
   a. to the point
   b. unspoken
   c. open
   d. friendly

9. terse
   a. unspoken
   b. frank
   c. brief
   d. a pardon

10. verbose
   a. quiet
   b. wordy
   c. brief
   d. friendly

LESSON 5

11. affluent
   a. result
   b. cause
   c. wealthy
   d. secret

12. alternative
   a. relating to something
   b. imaginary
   c. choice
   d. unfriendly

13. concise
   a. wordy
   b. to cut off
   c. choice
   d. brief

14. famish
   a. tired
   b. starved
   c. long
   d. food

15. fatigue
   a. hungry
   b. tired
   c. starved
   d. asleep

16. formidable
   a. of discouraging difficulty
   b. apathetic
   c. open
   b. inactive

17. mundane
a. healthy
b. uncaring
c. ordinary
d. friendly

18. nostalgic
a. nosy
b. friendly
c. noticeable
d. homesick

19. optimist
a. one who is bad
b. relating to something
c. one who is friendly
d. one who is cheerful

20. pessimist
a. one who is a pest
b. one who is gloomy
c. one who is friendly
d. one who is cheerful

LESSON 6

21. amnesty
a. short
b. a pardon
c. wordy
d. honest

22. covert
a. open
b. prying
c. concealed
d. spy

23. curtail
a. curious
b. to shorten
c. cheerful
d. inactive

24. fatal
a. poison
b. open
c. secret
d. causing death

25. fictitious
a. story
b. imaginary
c. real
d. unsophisticated

26. hostile
a. friendly
b. kill
c. unfriendly
d. hurt

27. lethal
a. poison
b. dangerous
c. hurt
d. deadly

28. overt
a. open
b. secret
c. closed
d. relating to something

29. relevant
a. friendly
b. secret
c. open
d. pertinent

30. sentimental
a. lacking feeling
b. emotional
c. sentence
d. friendly

STOP. *Check answers at the back of the book on page 243–244.*

LESSON 7

WORDS

aesthetic	affront	antagonize	attitude	characteristic
derogatory	euphemism	hypocrite	inclination	intimidate

1. **aesthetic** (es • thet′ ik) *adj.* Relating to beauty; sensitive to art and beauty; showing good taste; artistic.
   *People who are more sensitive to art and beauty have a more **aesthetic** sense than others have.*

2. **affront** (uh • front′) *v.* To insult. *n.* An insult; an open and intentional insult.
   *When everyone except me was invited to the party, I considered that a personal **affront**.*

3. **antagonize** (an • tag′ uh • nīz) *v.* To make unfriendly; to make an enemy of; to oppose; to act against.
   *If you continue to behave in the such a haughty way, you will **antagonize** everyone at school.*

4. **attitude** (at′ i • tūd) *n.* A way of feeling, acting, or thinking that shows one's disposition (frame of mind) or opinion; the feeling itself; posture.
   *It can be difficult to change our feelings about some things because our **attitudes** come from our past experiences and have been with us for awhile.*

5. **characteristic** (kar • ik • tuh • ris′ tik) *adj.* Marking the peculiar qualities of a person or thing; distinctive; special. *n.* A special trait, feature, or quality; individuality.
   *My friends and I decided that haughty people seem to share certain **characteristics**.*

6. **derogatory** (de • rog′ uh • tor • ē) *adj.* Tending to make less well regarded; tending to belittle someone or something; disparaging; belittling.
   *The **derogatory** remarks that our teammate made about Dave were supposed to make us think less of him, but they made us think less of the person who made them.*

7. **euphemism** (ū′ fuh • miz • um) *n.* The substitution of a word or phrase that is less direct, milder, or vaguer for one thought to be harsh, offensive, or blunt; a word or phrase considered less offensive or distasteful than another.
*Many of us use a **euphemism** when speaking of death, such as* They are in their final resting place *for* They are dead.

8. **hypocrite** (hip′ uh • krit) *n.* A person who pretends to be what he or she is not; one who pretends to be better than he or she actually is.
*What a **hypocrite** he is to make us feel guilty about wanting our share of the profits when he already has pocketed his share.*

9. **inclination** (in • kluh • nā′ shun) *n.* A personal leaning or bent; a liking; a bending; a sloping surface; a slope.
*We were able to figure out Jason's **inclination** for enjoying all kinds of sports when we saw how much time he spent at the gym.*

10. **intimidate** (in • tim′ uh • dāt) *v.* To make timid; to cause fear; to scare; to discourage by threats or violence.
*There always seem to be a few bullies who **intimidate** others smaller than they are.*

Practices

PRACTICE A

Directions: Choose a word from the list that *best* fits the blank in each sentence.

WORD LIST

aesthetic	affront	antagonize	attitude	characteristic
derogatory	euphemism	hypocrite	inclination	intimidate

1. A *regime change* is considered a(n) _____ for *overthrow of government*.

2. Because Kim is quite artistic, her _____ sense is highly developed.

3. When Jack was insulted by his brother, he took the _____ more to heart than if someone else had insulted him.

4. Have you noticed that some people go out of their way not to _____ others because they don't like to be enemies with anyone?

5. Why do many politicians have to make such _____ remarks about the person they are running against?

6. My feelings, that is, my _____ toward lots of things, are beginning to change since I've been away at school.

7. We learned about the special _____ of various animals in my biology class.

8. I get upset when some people at school try to _____ me by threatening to fight me.

9. Sue must be a(n) _____ because when she was in front of a group of people, she said that she would help us, but it now appears that she had no intention of doing so.

10. Carol told me that her _____ is to stay where she is, so I was surprised to hear that she is considering a move to another state.

> **STOP.** *Check answers at the back of the book on page 244.*

PRACTICE B

Directions: Match the word with the meaning that *best* fits.

Words	***Meanings***
_____ 1. antagonize	a. an insult
_____ 2. attitude	b. belittling
_____ 3. aesthetic	c. one's feelings
_____ 4. affront	d to make an enemy of
_____ 5. characteristic	e. a less distasteful word or phrase to describe something
_____ 6. derogatory	f. referring to beauty
_____ 7. euphemism	g. a personal leaning or bent
_____ 8. hypocrite	h. to make timid

_____ 9. inclination   i. one who pretends to be what he or she is not

_____ 10. intimidate   j. peculiar quality

STOP. *Check answers at the back of the book on page 244.*

PRACTICE C

Directions: Define the following words.

1. Aesthetic _____

2. Affront _____

3. Antagonize _____

4. Attitude _____

5. Characteristic _____

6. Derogatory _____

7. Euphemism _____

8. Hypocrite _____

9. Inclination _____

10. Intimidate _____

LESSON 8

WORDS

apprehensive	bland	discreet	docile	infamous
initiate	miscellaneous	omission	scrutinize	unanimous

1. **apprehensive** (ap • ri • hen′ siv) *adj.* Fearful; expecting evil, danger, or harm; anxious.
   *After the mischief that someone did to my dorm room, I was very **apprehensive** about leaving it.*

2. **bland** (bland) *adj.* Mild; soft; gentle; balmy; kindly; soothing.
   *Kathy only ate **bland** food such as soup after she had an upset stomach because it is gentle on the stomach.*

3. **discreet** (dis • krēt′) *adj.* Careful about what one says or does; prudent; cautious.
   *The family members of a powerful person should behave in a **discreet** manner so as not to embarrass their relative.*

4. **docile** (dos′ ul) *adj.* Easy to teach; easy to discipline; obedient; one easily led.
   *Most instructors like to have **docile** students in their class because they don't cause much trouble.*

5. **infamous** (in′ fuh • mus) *adj.* Notorious; having a bad reputation.
   *Some students at our school are **infamous** for their bad behavior.*

6. **initiate** (i • nish′ ē • āt) *v.* To introduce by doing or using first; to bring into use or practice; to admit as a member into a fraternity, sorority, club, and so on, especially through the use of a secret ceremony.
   *When I was chosen to join a sorority, the sisters told me that they had to **initiate** me first before I could become a regular member.*

7. **miscellaneous** (mis • uh • lā′ nē • us) *adj.* Mixed; consisting of several kinds; various.
   *I'd rather have a cafeteria food plan with a **miscellaneous** menu than one that limits my options.*

8. **omission** (ō • mish′ un) *n.* Anything left out or not done; failure to include.
   *You can imagine how upset I was during graduation when the college president made the **omission** of not calling my name.*

9. **scrutinize** (skrūt′ un • īz) *v.* To observe closely; to examine or inquire into critically; to investigate.
   *The college president said that she would **scrutinize** the graduation procedure to determine why my name had been omitted.*

10. **unanimous** (ū • nan′ uh • mus) *adj.* Agreeing completely; united in opinion; being of one mind; being in complete agreement.
    *Because everyone was in agreement, the decision was a **unanimous** one.*

Practices

PRACTICE A

Directions: Choose a word from the word list that *best* fits the blank in each sentence.

WORD LIST

apprehensive	bland	discreet	docile	infamous
initiate	miscellaneous	omission	scrutinize	unanimous

1. One student in our school is _____ for his disrespectful behavior.

2. Our instructors prefer _____ students to those who enjoy disrupting the class.

3. After a recent mugging on campus, most of us became _____ about walking home alone at night.

4. Most of us are _____ when we are told not to discuss exams that other students haven't taken yet.

5. Some students refer to our instructor as a mild or _____ person, but others claim that she isn't as uninteresting as she seems.

6. On the first day of drama class, our instructor likes to _____ the students into the class by having each one introduce himself or herself by singing a song or telling a joke.

7. Our instructor told us we could pick an assignment either from a list of specific topics or from a list of _____ ones.

8. The _____ of my name from the class list last semester caused me a lot of grief.

9. I carefully _____ my course syllabus at the beginning of every semester to make sure I don't miss any important assignments.

10. Because everyone agreed, the decision was _____.

> **STOP.** *Check answers at the back of the book on page 244.*

PRACTICE B

Directions: Match the word with the meaning that *best* fits.

	Words	Meanings
_____	1. apprehensive	a. agreeing completely
_____	2. bland	b. to investigate
_____	3. discreet	c. fearful
_____	4. docile	d. failure to include
_____	5. infamous	e. to introduce
_____	6. initiate	f. notorious
_____	7. miscellaneous	g. mild
_____	8. omission	h. mixed
_____	9. scrutinize	i. obedient
_____	10. unanimous	j. cautious

> **STOP.** *Check answers at the back of the book on page 244.*

PRACTICE C

Directions: Define the following words.

1. Apprehensive _____

2. Bland _____

3. Discreet _____

4. Docile _____

5. Infamous _____

6. Initiate _____

7. Miscellaneous _____

8. Omission _____

9. Scrutinize _____

10. Unanimous _____

LESSON 9

WORDS

acquisition	adept	adversary	anecdote	contagious
curt	paradox	subsequent	variable	versatile

1. **acquisition** (ak • wi • zish′ un) *n.* The act of obtaining or acquiring; something obtained or gained as property, knowledge, and so on.
   *When the school population increased, the **acquisition** of another building was necessary to house all the students.*

2. **adept** (uh • dept′) *adj.* Highly skilled; proficient; expert.
   *Because José is so **adept** in golf, he will probably receive an athletic scholarship to a university.*

3. **adversary** (ad′ vur • ser • ē) *n.* Enemy; one who opposes another, as in battle or debate; one who acts against someone or something; antagonist; opponent.
   *At college, the person running against me for a council seat has been my **adversary** since the first grade.*

4. **anecdote** (an′ ek • dōt) *n.* A short entertaining account of some happening, usually personal or biographical.
   *During the school election, I noticed that the students paid more attention to me if I told a humorous **anecdote** from my childhood.*

5. **contagious** (kun • tā′ jus) *adj.* Spreading by contact; spreading or tending to spread from person to person.
   *Jeb's laughter was so **contagious** that soon all of us were laughing hysterically.*

6. **curt** (kurt) *adj.* Rude; short; to the point.
   *We were all surprised to hear mild-mannered Beth speak in such a **curt** manner to Jason.*

7. **paradox** (par' uh • doks) *n.* Contradiction; a self-contradictory statement that is false; a statement that seems absurd, contradictory, or unbelievable but may be true.

*It is a **paradox** to claim to be here and not here at the same time.*

8. **subsequent** (sub' suh • kwent) *adj.* Following soon after; following in time, place, or order; resulting.

*In this book, Lesson 9 is **subsequent** to Lesson 8; that is, it follows Lesson 8.*

9. **variable** (var' ēuh • bul) *adj.* Changeable. *n.* Something that may or does change or vary.

*We don't know what to wear to the game because the weather has been so **variable**.*

10. **versatile** (ver' suh • tīl) *adj.* Turning with ease from one thing to another; able to do many things well; many-sided; having many uses.

*Fortunately for our team, our star player was **versatile** enough to play many positions.*

Practices

PRACTICE A

Directions: Choose a word from the word list that *best* fits the blank in each sentence.

WORD LIST

acquisition	adept	adversary	anecdote	contagious
curt	paradox	subsequent	variable	versatile

1. Jack, our star quarterback, is a very _____ player who can do many things well.

2. He is quite _____ at everything he does.

3. There is a(n) _____ going around campus about how he helped us win an important game.

4. _____ to that game, most team players listened carefully to the coach when he told them about how Jack helped win an important game for them.

5. It seems that Jack's desire to win was _____ because the rest of the players really exerted themselves after his efforts.

6. Most of us at school couldn't believe that Jack used to be a mean and _____ fellow because he is so polite and mild-mannered now; it seems like a(n) _____ to us.

7. We were told that years ago, he used to play for another school and was considered a formidable _____.

8. It seems that one of our coaches saw him play and talked him into transferring to our school; it was the best _____ that the coach ever made.

9. Let's hope that the good weather holds up for our next game because it has been so _____ lately.

> **STOP.** *Check answers at the back of the book on page 244.*

PRACTICE B

Directions: Match the word with the meaning that *best* fits.

Words	*Meanings*
_____ 1. acquisition	a. expert
_____ 2. adept	b. changeable
_____ 3. adversary	c. following
_____ 4. anecdote	d. contradiction
_____ 5. contagious	e. many-sided
_____ 6. curt	f. act of acquiring
_____ 7. paradox	g. enemy
_____ 8. subsequent	h. short, entertaining story
_____ 9. variable	i. spreading from person to person
_____ 10. versatile	j. impolite

> **STOP.** *Check answers at the back of the book on page 244.*

PRACTICE C

Directions: Define the following words.

1. Acquisition _____

2. Adept _____

3. Adversary _____

4. Anecdote _____

5. Contagious _____

6. Curt _____

7. Paradox _____

8. Subsequent _____

9. Variable _____

10. Versatile _____

Multiple-Choice Assessment of Lessons 7–9

Directions: Words are arranged by lesson. Underline the meaning that *best* fits the word. Answers are at the back of the book. **If you miss any word meaning, go back to the lesson and restudy the word.**

LESSON 7

1. aesthetic
a. referring to being poor
b. referring to beauty
c. likes food
d. a feeling

2. affront
a. an insult
b. friendly
c. a front
d. not friendly

3. antagonize
a. helpful
b. to make an enemy of
c. friendly
d. feeling

4. attitude
a. manner of feeling
b. friendly feeling
c. unfriendly feeling
d. happy feeling

5. characteristic
a. person
b. special trait
c. play
d. feeling

6. derogatory
a. a lot of
b. helpful
c. tending to belittle
d. talkative

7. euphemism
a. a wise saying
b. a saying
c. to belittle
d. a less distasteful description
   of something

8. hypocrite
a. to frighten
b. to lean
c. to be friendly
d. one who pretends to be
   something he or she is not

9. inclination
a. insult
b. frighten
c. a leaning
d. a saying

10. intimidate
a. to scare
b. to insult
c. to lean
d. to make unfriendly

LESSON 8

11. apprehensive
a. mild
b. helpful
c. fearful
d. cheerful

12. bland
a. refers to sadness
b. mild
c. friendly
d. evil

13. discreet
a. fearful
b. friendly
c. careful
d. evil

14. docile
a. active
b. easy to reach
c. noisy
d. easy to teach

15. infamous
a. well known
b. a crook
c. happy
d. having a bad reputation

16. initiate
a. to party
b. to insult
c. to start
d. to frighten

17. miscellaneous
a. mixed
b. wrong
c. most
d. one

18. omission
a. task
b. trip
c. skill
d. anything left out

19. scrutinize
a. able to see
b. to observe very closely
c. to watch someone
d. to read

20. unanimous
a. agreeing completely
b. several
c. some
d. not any

LESSON 9

21. acquisition
a. curious
b. quiet
c. inquisitive
d. the obtaining of something

22. adept
a. helpful
b. proficient
c. friendly
d. changing

23. adversary
   a. friend
   b. enemy
   c. opposite
   d. ally

24. anecdote
   a. something funny
   b. a joke
   c. a note
   d. an entertaining account
      of something

25. contagious
   a. germs
   b. spreading from person
      to person
   c. referring to contact
   d. unhealthy

26. curt
   a. impolite
   b. polite
   c. friendly
   d. heavy

27. paradox
   a. friendly
   b. healthy
   c. contradiction
   d. even

28. subsequent
   a. before
   b. after
   c. follow
   d. following after

29. variable
   a. changeable
   b. turning
   c. many-sided
   d. refers to weather

30. versatile
   a. useful
   b. many-sided
   c. ease
   d. turning

STOP. Check answers at the back of the book on page 244.

WORDS

appraise	domestic	exotic	gregarious	irate
mimic	oxymoron	passive	trite	turmoil

1. **appraise** (uh • prāz′) *v.* To judge the quality or value of; to set a price for.
   *My grandmother asked a realtor to **appraise** her house.*

2. **domestic** (dō • mes′ tik) *adj.* Having to do with the home; one's own country or referring to one's own country. *n.* A servant.
   *My friends at school claim that they prefer **domestic** products to foreign ones.*

3. **exotic** (eg • zot′ ik) *adj.* Foreign; charmingly unfamiliar; not native; strangely beautiful.
   *George had the florist import the **exotic** plant that he gave to his girlfriend.*

4. **gregarious** (gri • gar′ ē • us) *adj.* Fond of the company of others; sociable; characteristic of a flock, herd, or crowd.
   *My **gregarious** friends at school always plan a party for Saturday night.*

5. **irate** (ī • rāt′) *adj.* Angry; wrathful.
   *We all became **irate** when we heard that our friend had been expelled from school for what we thought was no good reason.*

6. **mimic** (mim′ ik) *n.* A person or thing that imitates. *v.* To imitate. *adj.* Imitative; inclined to copy.
   *Even though it's not nice to **mimic** another person's speech, some people will do it to get a laugh.*

7. **oxymoron** (oks • ē • mōr′ an) *n.* A figure of speech in which opposite or contradictory terms are combined.
   *Molly used **oxymorons,** such as the* living dead *and the* dawn of night *in her paper on vampires to make her writing more interesting.*

8. passive (pa′ siv) *adj.* Inactive; unresisting; not opposing; unenthusiastic.

*When I have no interest in a class discussion, I look outwardly **passive** and quiet, but I inside I am actively counting the minutes until class is over.*

9. trite (trīt) *adj.* Made commonplace by repetition; used so often as to make it too common; lacking originality or freshness.

*Our professor liked the way I used oxymorons in my paper, but he said to choose them carefully, because some oxymorons were becoming **trite** from overuse.*

10. turmoil (tur′ moil) *n.* Disturbance; confused motion or state; tumult.

*Right before the holidays, there's usually a lot of **turmoil** on campus because students are getting ready to go home for vacation.*

Practices

PRACTICE A

Directions: Choose a word from the word list that *best* fits the blank in each sentence.

WORD LIST

appraise	domestic	exotic	gregarious	irate
mlmic	oxymoron	passive	trite	turmoil

1. I prefer to buy _____ fruit and vegetables rather than fruit and vegetables from overseas.

2. I, however, love to buy _____ flowers that come from overseas for my significant other.

3. Is it a(n) _____ to say "big little girl"?

4. When we were told that we had to move from our apartment immediately, we became quite _____.

5. Our landlady said she had heard that we would _____ the way she and her and visitors spoke.

6. We are not the kind of people who would make fun of other people, so we felt that she was using a(n) _____ reason to get rid of us.

7. Our move would cause a lot of _____ for us, so we reminded our landlady that we had signed a lease and that she needed to give us 30 days' notice if she wanted us to leave.

8. We are usually fairly _____ about most things, but we became annoyed about having to leave our quarters in the middle of the school semester.

9. Our landlady wouldn't return our deposit for the apartment because she said the person she hired to _____ the apartment after we vacated claimed that we had left it in a mess.

10. My _____ roommate, who is usually quite aggressive and outspoken, said that rather than arguing with our landlady, we should go to small claims court and have our dispute settled there.

STOP. *Check the answers at the back of the book on page 244.*

PRACTICE B

Directions: Match the word with the meaning that *best* fits.

	Words	*Meanings*
_____	1. appraise	a. foreign
_____	2. domestic	b. to judge the value of
_____	3. exotic	c. having to do with home
_____	4. gregarious	d. disturbance
_____	5. irate	e. outgoing
_____	6. mimic	f. angry
_____	7. oxymoron	g. inactive
_____	8. passive	h. imitate
_____	9. trite	i. figure of speech using opposites
_____	10. turmoil	j. lacking freshness

STOP. *Check answers at the back of the book on page 244.*

PRACTICE C

Directions: Choose the word from the word list that *best* fits in the blank. A word may be used once only. If necessary, you may change the form of the word in the word list.

WORD LIST

appraise	domestic	exotic	gregarious	irate
mimic	oxymoron	passive	trite	turmoil

Gregory has a lot of personality and is a very (1)_____ person. He likes to try to make people laugh, but at times, he goes too far. For example, last Economics class, he thought that he would poke fun at our instructor's British accent by (2)_____ him. He had done this so many times before that many people thought it was getting (3)_____. But some (4)_____ students who don't like to cause a commotion felt that Gregory caused a(n) (5)_____ because our instructor walked in while Gregory was in the midst of his act. At that moment, we knew the meaning of the (6)_____ "a loud silence." Our instructor did not become (7)_____, but he had every right to be. Instead, he ignored Gregory and started to talk about the attraction of (8)_____ items from other countries versus (9)_____ things we can get in our country. He told us we would have a quiz on the unit to (10)_____ how well we learned the material.

11

WORDS

apprise	compromise	conform	crass	emulate
plaintiff	pretense	tact	traditional	wary

1. **apprise** (uh • prīz′) *v.* To inform or notify.
   *Many students confuse the words "appraise," which refers to placing a value on something, and **apprise**, which means to notify or inform.*

2. **compromise** (kum′ pruh • mīz) *v.* To settle or adjust by both sides making some concessions. *n.* The making of adjustments to settle something by both sides giving something; something midway between two things.
   *Both sides were unhappy with the **compromise**, but it was certainly better than what presently existed.*

3. **conform** (cun • form′) *v.* To make the same or similar; to behave in a conventional way without questioning, especially in accepting customs, opinions, and so on.
   *Although many students claim that they want to be individuals, they still **conform** and wear the same clothes as everyone else.*

4. **crass** (cras) *adj.* Dull; grossly stupid; insensitive; tasteless and coarse; blatantly materialistic; money grubbing.
   *My friends do not like **crass** people who are always bragging about their latest purchases.*

5. **emulate** (em′ ū • lāt) *v.* To imitate or copy; to try to equal by imitating. To often imitate or copy an admired person.
   *In the way she dressed, Mary would often try to **emulate** pop stars such as Britney Spears.*

6. **plaintiff** (plān′ tif) *n.* A person who brings a suit into a court of law; the complainant.
   On court dramas such as Law and Order, *the **plaintiff** is usually represented by an assistant district attorney.*

7. pretense (prē • tens') *n*. A false claim; a usually unsupported claim concerning an accomplishment; a pretending; make believe.

*My buddies and I were really taken in by Bob's **pretense** of having been famous at his former school.*

8. tact (takt) *n*. Skill in dealing with people; seeming to know the right thing to say and do so as not to offend someone.

*Because Sharon and her sister Carol both have such great **tact**, they would make good counselors.*

9. traditional (truh • dish' uh • nul) *adj*. Conforming to tradition; conventional.

*Our school is a very **traditional** one that conforms to the customs of the town in which it is situated.*

10. wary (war' ē) *adj*. Cautious; careful.

*We were taught at an early age to be **wary** of strangers, especially those who offered us a lift.*

Practices

PRACTICE A

Directions: Choose a word from the word list that *best* fits the blank in each sentence.

WORD LIST

apprise	compromise	conform	crass	emulate
plaintiff	pretense	tact	traditional	wary

1. After my sister was mugged on campus, she became very _____ about walking alone late at night.

2. When neither side could agree on a plan for the party, we decided that it was time to _____.

3. Jim said that he would _____ us of everything that went on at the meeting.

4. My parents are conventional, that is, _____ people, so they became upset when I refused to _____ to their way of thinking and doing things.

5. At school, I am known for my _____ but somehow when it comes to dealing with my parents, I just lose my cool.

6. My mother especially had hoped that I would _____ her and also become a lawyer.

7. My mother had visions of the two of us opening up a law firm and working with _____ who wanted to bring their cases to court.

8. I consider it _____ to be paid to represent people whose cases probably do not have much merit.

9. For a short time, I thought that I would be what my parents wanted, but I couldn't keep up the _____.

> **STOP.** *Check answers at the back of the book on page 244.*

PRACTICE B

Directions: Define the following words.

1. Apprise _____

2. Compromise _____

3. Conform _____

4. Crass _____

5. Emulate _____

6. Plaintiff _____

7. Pretense _____

8. Tact _____

9. Traditional _____

10. Wary _____

STOP. *Check answers at the back of the book on page 244.*

PRACTICE C

Directions: Choose the word from the word list that *best* fits in the blank. A word may be used once only. If necessary, you may change the form of the word.

WORD LIST

apprise	compromise	conform	crass	emulate
plaintiff	pretense	tact	traditional	wary

Pam and I have been friends since kindergarten. We presently are taking many of the same classes at college. If either one of us is absent we (1)_____ each other of what we missed. Pam is nice—there are no (2)_____ about her. She always says, "What you see is what you get." Pam also has lots of (3)_____. She will never deliberately hurt anyone's feelings. She (4)_____ people she admires. Even though she has been brought up with old-fashioned manners and is pretty (5)_____ in her outlook, she will not try to push you to her views. To keep the peace, she always seems to be the one to (6)_____ on many issues. She doesn't care much about money—I don't believe there is a(n) (7)_____ bone in her body. In addition, she is (8)_____ of people who say one thing and do another. You can imagine my surprise when she said that she disagreed with the student council jury for dismissing the (9)_____ charge that another student had not (10)_____ to the school rules.

12

WORDS

assumption	assurance	awry	expend	extricate
gullible	inevitable	infidelity	remorse	spouse

1. assumption (uh • sump' shun) *n.* The act of taking for granted without proof; a taking to or upon oneself; a supposition.

*When one of my buddies was caught illegally copying material from the Internet, some students on campus made the wrong **assumption** that everyone does it.*

2. assurance (uh • shur' ans) *n.* The act of making sure or certain; security; certainty; confidence; guarantee.

*Jim initially denied illegally copying material from the Internet, and most people believed him because he spoke with such **assurance**.*

3. awry (uh • rī') *adj.* or *adv.* With a turn or twist to one side; away from the expected or hoped for direction; wrong.

*When Jim first handed in his paper, things were going smoothly him, but once he was caught cheating, his plans for an easy "A" went **awry**.*

4. expend (ek • spend') *v.* To use up; to spend.

*Jim should have done the project the right way, because in spite of his cheating, he did **expend** a lot of energy on it.*

5. extricate (eks' truh • kāt) *v.* To free or release from difficulties, entanglements, embarrassing situations, and so on.

*Jim knew that the longer he waited to tell his instructor about copying the paper from the Internet, the more difficult it would be for him to **extricate** himself from the situation, but he seemed powerless to act.*

6. gullible (gul' uh • bul) *adj.* Easily deceived or cheated.

*Jim thought he could take advantage of his instructor because she was so young and **gullible**; he thought she would believe everything he told her.*

7. **inevitable** (in • ev′ i • tuh • bul) *adj.* Not able to be avoided or escaped; sure to happen; certain.
*Jim led such a dangerous life that it was **inevitable** he would get caught in something he was trying to pull.*

8. **infidelity** (in • fuh • del′ uh • tē) *n.* Unfaithfulness; adultery; a disloyal act.
*Jim may be a faithful friend to his buddies, but his girlfriend has caught him in countless acts of **infidelity**.*

9. **remorse** (ri • mors′) *n.* Painful and deep regret for wrongdoing; a strong anguish arising from regret for past deeds.
*When Jim was reproached for his wrongdoing, he said that he was filled with **remorse** and that he would change his ways, but somehow no one believed him.*

10. **spouse** (spouz) *n.* A husband or wife; either member of a married pair.
*At night my roommate and I often talk about whether our current boyfriends would make us a good **spouse**.*

Practices

PRACTICE A

Directions: Choose a word from the word list that *best* fits the definition.

WORD LIST

assumption	assurance	awry	expend	extricate
gullible	inevitable	infidelity	remorse	spouse

1. Away from the expected direction _____

2. To use up _____

3. A husband or wife _____

4. To free or release from difficulty _____

5. The act of making sure _____

6. Unfaithfulness _____

7. Painful and deep regret for wrongdoing _____

8. The act of taking for granted without proof _____

9. Certain; sure to happen _____

10. Easily deceived _____

> **STOP.** *Check answers at the back of the book on page 244.*

PRACTICE B

Directions: Define the *italicized* word in each sentence.

1. We have no *assurance* that you will not again allow minors to enter the premises; therefore we will not grant you a permit to reopen. _____

   _____

2. In most houses today, both *spouses* seem to share equally in decisionmaking.

   _____

3. I can't afford to *expend* any more of my time or energy on this project.

   _____

4. When the driver learned that while driving under the influence of alcohol, he had hit and crippled a small child, he felt great *remorse* and said that he would never drink another drop again. _____

5. Each day, she seemed to get deeper and deeper into debt to the loan sharks; soon she would find it impossible to *extricate* herself from their clutches.

   _____

6. The officer at the bank refused to speak to the poorly dressed man because he was under the *assumption* that the man was not very important; however, the unkempt customer turned out to be one of the bank's best accounts.

   _____

7. It was a shock to Sara when she learned about her spouse's *infidelity*.

   _____

8. When my plans go *awry*, I stop to figure out what went wrong.

   _____

9. Most people agree that the two things that are *inevitable* in life are death and taxes. _____

10. My *gullible* friend now holds shares in two dry oil wells, a piece of swamp land, and a nonexistent company. _____

> **STOP.** *Check answers at the back of the book on page 244.*

PRACTICE C

Directions: Choose the word from the word list that *best* fits in the blank. A word may be used once only. If necessary, you may also change the form of the word in the word list.

WORD LIST

assumption	assurance	awry	expend	extricate
gullible	inevitable	infidelity	remorse	spouse

Dina and her (1)_____, Fred, have been married for five years. When they first got married, they made the (2)_____ that they would always be in love. They looked at both their sets of parents, who together had been married for almost a century. This gave them the (3)_____ they needed to commit to marriage. Dina and Fred now say that they were quite (4)_____ and believed all the fairy tales about "happily ever after" when they first got married. They could not imagine anything going (5)_____ in their marriage or would have predicted that just five years later they would want to (6)_____ themselves from it. Both Dina and Fred claim that they (7)_____ a lot of energy to keep their marriage going. Neither one had been unfaithful, but (8)_____ was always on their minds. They both have (9)_____ about their separation and upcoming divorce. They realized, however, that the bloom was off their marriage and it was (10)_____ that they would separate.

Multiple-Choice Assessment of Lessons 10–12

Directions: Words are arranged by lesson. Underline the meaning that *best* fits the word. Answers are at the back of the book. **If you miss any word meaning, go back to the lesson and restudy the word.**

LESSON 10

1. **appraise**
   a. to praise
   b. to acclaim
   c. to be worthy of
   d. to estimate the value of

2. **domestic**
   a. referring to the home
   b. foreign
   c. something like cheese
   d. a person

3. exotic
  a. foreign
  b. home
  c. goods exported
  d. a flower

4. gregarious
  a. unfriendly
  b. a herd
  c. outgoing
  d. wild

5. irate
  a. irritation
  b. angry
  c. yelling
  d. fighting

6. mimic
  a. to think about
  b. a clown
  c. to imitate
  d. a performer

7. oxymoron
  a. contradictory ideas
  b. stupid
  c. dumb concepts
  d. a person with below average
     intelligence

8. passive
  a. enthusiastic
  b. unresisting
  c. lively
  d. active

9. trite
  a. important
  b. different
  c. meaningful
  d. commonplace

10. turmoil
  a. movement
  b. spirit
  c. confused motion
  d. lively

LESSON 11

11. apprise
  a. to inform
  b. to value
  c. to help
  d. to desire

12. compromise
  a. to give in
  b. to give up
  c. to settle
  d. to settle by mutual concession

13. conform
  a. to adapt oneself to
  b. to regulate
  c. to make rules
  d. to adapt others to

14. crass
  a. tired
  b. insensitive
  c. sensitive
  d. slow

15. emulate
  a. to regulate
  b. to imitate
  c. to prepare for
  d. to try

16. plaintiff
  a. a complaining person
  b. a friendly person
  c. the defendant
  d. the complaining person in
     a lawsuit

17. pretense
   a. a false claim
   b. one who hides
   c. a secret claim
   d. an unusual claim

18. tact
   a. skillful
   b. an expert
   c. skill in dealing with people
   d. ability to do many things

19. traditional
   a. reactionary
   b. ancient
   c. conventional
   d. contemporary

20. wary
   a. cautious
   b. secretive
   c. scared
   d. believable

LESSON 12

21. assumption
   a. the act of taking for granted
      with facts
   b. the act of taking
   c. the act of proving
   d. the act of taking for granted
      without proof

22. assurance
   a. insecurity
   b. certainty
   c. a policy
   d. an insurance claim

23. awry
   a. clever humor
   b. turning
   c. away from the expected direction
   d. the hoped-for direction

24. expend
   a. to quit
   b. to spend a lot of money
   c. to tire
   d. to use up

25. extricate
   a. to free from difficulties
   b. to escape
   c. to cut out
   d. to endure difficulties

26. gullible
   a. interesting
   b. easily cheated
   c. frightened
   d. able to be made to laugh

27. inevitable
   a. certain
   b. able to try
   c. not too certain
   d. not able to happen

28. infidelity
   a. a divorce
   b. a battle between spouses
   c. a separation
   d. unfaithfulness

29. remorse
   a. hope
   b. wrongdoing
   c. regret for past misdeeds
   d. atoning for sins

30. spouse
   a. relative
   b. a parent
   c. a brother or sister
   d. a husband or wife

STOP. *Check answers at the back of the book on page 244.*

LESSON 13

WORDS

anticipate	astute	charisma	cope	duration
idealist	motivate	reality	skeptical	tedious

1. anticipate (an • tis′ uh • pāt) *v.* To expect; to look forward to; to foresee; to act, use, or make in advance.

*From Selina's answers, you could tell that she **anticipated** exactly what questions the reporters would ask.*

2. astute (uh • stūt′) *adj.* Shrewd; ingenious; clever; crafty.

*The **astute** lawyer was able to win every argument.*

3. charisma (kuh • riz′ muh) *n.* A rare power or personal magic of leadership a person possesses that arouses special loyalty or enthusiasm from others; a special magnetic charm or appeal.

*The man running for office had such **charisma** that he didn't have any difficulty getting people to help him win the election.*

4. cope (kōp) *v.* To deal with and overcome problems and difficulties; to struggle or fight with on fairly even terms or with some degree of success.

*Selina was concerned that she wouldn't be able to **cope** with all the added job responsibilities if she were promoted.*

5. duration (du • rā′ shun) *n.* Persistence or continuance in time; the time during which something exists or lasts.

*For the **duration** of the strike, people had to find alternate means of transportation.*

6. idealist (ī • dē′ uh • list) *n.* A person who conforms to ultimate perfection or excellence; someone who acts according to high ideals; one who is unrealistic and impractical; one who believes in something that exists only in the mind.

*It's hard to be an **idealist** in a world filled with imperfection, but David is.*

7. motivate (mōt′ uh • vāt) *v.* To stimulate to action; to provide with an incentive; to set in motion or arouse.

*Our instructors use different techniques to **motivate** us to pay attention in class.*

8. reality (rē • al′ uh • tē) *n.* The state of being real, actual, or true; what actually exists or is.

*Some people distort **reality** to deal with their problems because they cannot face the situation as it is.*

9. skeptical (skep′ tuh • kul) *adj.* Inclined to doubt; not believing easily; questioning the truth of theories or facts.

*We were **skeptical** when Lisa told us that if we followed her advice, she would make us all wealthy overnight.*

10. tedious (tē′ dē • us) *adj.* Tiresome; boring; uninteresting because of extreme length or slowness; monotonous; wearisome.

*Erin considers her present position **tedious**, but we think she has an interesting job.*

Practices

PRACTICE A

Directions: Choose a word from the word list that *best* fits the definition.

WORD LIST

anticipate	astute	charisma	cope	duration
idealist	motivate	reality	skeptical	tedious

1. To stimulate to action _____

2. Inclined to doubt _____

3. One who is unrealistic _____

4. The time during which something lasts _____

5. Shrewd _____

6. Tiresome _____

7. To expect _____

8. To deal with _____

9. The state of being actual _____

10. A special magnetic charm or appeal _____

> **STOP.** *Check the answers at the end of the book on page 245.*

PRACTICE B

Directions: Choose a word from the word list that *best* fits the blank in each sentence.

WORD LIST

anticipate	astute	charisma	cope	duration
idealist	motivate	reality	skeptical	tedious

1. Working in a political campaign may seem exciting to outsiders, but it is actually very _____ work because all we do is stuff envelopes.

2. One of the candidates had to withdraw from the race because he had several major problems and he just could not _____ with them.

3. Sharon said that she does not _____ any problems with her new position.

4. Her _____ is so strong that she can get you to do practically anything for her.

5. After all the things that have happened in Carol's life, we couldn't believe that she could still be such a(n) _____.

6. The _____ man carefully evaluated his situation and knew that he would have to remain calm to get out alive.

7. For the _____ of this semester, I intend to do all my assignments and study for exams.

8. My friends are _____ about my keeping my vow to apply myself to my assignments because they know how much I hate to do school work.

9. This semester I am facing _____, so I see things the way they really are rather than as I would like them to be.

10. No one else can _____ you to do something unless you want to do it because the drive and energy must come from within you.

> **STOP.** *Check the answers at the back of the book on page 245.*

PRACTICE C

Directions: Choose the word from the word list that *best* fits in the blank. A word may be used once only. If necessary, you may also change the form of the word in the word list.

WORD LIST

anticipate	astute	charisma	cope	duration
idealist	motivate	reality	skeptical	tedious

My parents are (1)_____, and they expect me to conform to their sense of excellence. It's not surprising that when I was in college, my parents were somewhat (2)_____ when I told them that my friends were (3)_____ about planning their future, because none of them seemed particularly interested in anything but the here and now. They also didn't find my friends especially charming or (4)_____ and didn't understand what drew me to them. My parents felt that my friends never had to (5)_____ with any difficult problems. Consequently, they believed that my friends did not face (6)_____. Knowing my parents' beliefs, my friends had (7)_____ that my parents would feel the way they did toward them. In spite of my parents' objections, I remained friends with the group for the (8)_____ of my years at college. After leaving school, however, I began to find that many of their antics were (9)_____. I was no longer (10)_____ to behave in the same way.

14

WORDS

citation	cognitive	comprehensive	concept	objective
paraphrase	plagiarism	protagonist	subjective	synopsis

1. **citation** (sī • tā′ shun) *n.* The quoting of a passage, author, book, and so on; a quotation or reference given as an authority for facts, opinions, and so on; an official summons to appear before a court.
*When I write a paper for school, I use several **citations** from well-known authorities to back up my theories.*

2. **cognitive** (kog′ nuh • tiv) *adj.* Having to do with thinking.
*Reading is a **cognitive** act.*

3. **comprehensive** (kom • pruh • hen′ siv) *adj.* Of large scope; broad; including much; in insurance, covering or providing broad protection against loss.
*Our instructor said that our final exam would be a **comprehensive** one that would include the whole semester's work.*

4. **concept** (kon′ sept) *n.* Idea; a thought or notion.
*A **concept** is an abstraction and is not something that is concrete or can be touched.*

5. **objective** (ob • jek′ tiv) *n.* Purpose; goal; aim; something that one is attempting to achieve. *adj.* Unbiased; not affected by personal feelings or prejudice; based on facts; having to do with a material object rather than with something mental such as an idea or concept. Something that can be directly observed.
*It is very difficult for anyone to be completely **objective** because no one is totally free from some kind of bias.*

6. **paraphrase** (par′ uh • frāz) *n.* A rewording of a passage; a restatement of a text or passage giving the meaning in another form or to make the meaning more clear. *v.* To reword or restate something, usually for clarity.
*Our instructor told us that we need to give citations even when we **paraphrase** another person's work in a paper we are writing.*

7. plagiarism (plā′ juh • riz • um) *n.* The act of taking the thoughts, writing, inventions, and so on of another and presenting them as your own.

*Even though the Internet has made it easier for students to download reports and pass them off as their own, there are Web sites that instructors can use to find those who have resorted to this type of **plagiarism**.*

8. protagonist (prō • tag′ uh • nist) *n.* The main character in a novel, story, or play; the leader of a cause or movement.

*In the play, the **protagonist** was a strong character who seemed to control the destiny of all who came in contact with her.*

9. subjective (sub • jek′ tiv) *adj.* Existing in the mind; personal; individual thought; influenced by a person's state of mind.

***Subjective** tests such as essay exams have more than one correct answer, making them more difficult to grade than objective exams, which have one answer only.*

10. synopsis (si • nop′ sis) *n.* A brief statement giving a general view of a passage, story, play, and so forth; a summary.

*My English literature professor requires us to write a **synopsis** of the ten plays that we read in his course.*

Practices

PRACTICE A

Directions: Choose a word from the word list that *best* fits the definition.

WORD LIST

citation	cognitive	comprehensive	concept	objective
paraphrase	plagiarism	protagonist	subjective	synopsis

1. The main character in a story _____

2. Existing in the mind _____

3. Idea _____

4. The quoting of a passage _____

5. A summary _____

6. Of broad scope _____

7. A restatement of a passage _____

8. Presenting another's writings as one's own _____

9. Having to do with thinking _____

10. Based on facts _____

> **STOP.** *Check answers at the end of the book on page 245.*

PRACTICE B

Directions: Choose a word from the word list that *best* fits the blank in each sentence.

WORD LIST

citation	cognitive	comprehensive	concept	objective
paraphrase	plagiarism	protagonist	subjective	synopsis

1. A person who has had brain damage might have difficulty working in areas that require _____ ability.

2. That is one of the most _____ reports that I have ever seen because it seems to cover everything.

3. My friends prefer essay exams, because these _____ types of tests have more than one right answer.

4. I prefer _____ tests such as multiple-choice ones in which there is one correct answer.

5. The _____ in the novel was a young man who had difficulty relating to his parents; after they died, however, he gained a better understanding of them.

6. When you write a short _____ of a story, give the story's main idea as well as the most important details that develop the main idea.

7. Most auto makers come up with _____ cars to display at auto shows that include design features they may put on actual cars in the future.

8. We were all surprised when an honor student handed in a paper with falsified _____.

9. She had gone to the Internet and downloaded someone else's work, but our instructor sent all our papers to a special Web site that specializes in detecting _____.

10. The assignment wasn't a hard one because our instructor showed us how to _____ material in our own words and how to cite such material.

> **STOP.** *Check answers at the back of the book on page 245.*

PRACTICE C

Directions: Choose the word from the word list that *best* fits in the blank. A word may be used once only. If necessary, you may change the form of the word in the word list.

WORD LIST

citation	cognitive	comprehensive	concept	objective
paraphrase	plagiarism	protagonist	subjective	synopsis

My English professor's (1)_____ of a short paper is about 20 pages. She wants my class to write a(n) (2)_____ 20-page essay analyzing the motives of the (3)_____ from one of the books we have read. First, she wants us to write a short (4)_____ of the book. She said that she expects a lot of (5)_____ in our choice of books. We should, however, try to be as (6)_____ as we can when we discuss the character. She wants us to use our (7)_____ skills to come up with a thought-provoking analysis. If we go to the Internet to research the character, we should be careful not to (8)_____ someone else's work, and when we (9)_____ someone else's ideas into our own words, we should be sure to include the (10)_____ for whatever we have put into our own words.

15

WORDS

compatible	discord	dogmatic	dominant	durable
exceedingly	harmony	literally	prestige	status

1. **compatible** (kum • pat' uh • bul) *adj.* Able to exist together; capable of living in an agreeable manner with another; able to get on well with another; capable of orderly operation and integration with other elements in a system; consistent.
   *Next semester, I am going to room with someone else because my current roommate and I are not **compatible**.*

2. **discord** (dis' kord) *n.* Lack of agreement among people, groups, or things; difference of opinion; dispute; dissention; disagreement; a confused or harsh mingling of sounds; a din.
   *If there is a great amount of **discord** between spouses, the marriage usually ends in a divorce.*

3. **dogmatic** (dog • mat' ik) *adj.* Asserting opinions as if they were fact; excessively positive in asserting opinions; opinionated.
   *It is difficult to discuss anything with a **dogmatic** person, because that person is not interested in another point of view.*

4. **dominant** (dom' uh • nant) *adj.* Ruling; most influential; controlling; exerting authority or influence; a commanding position.
   *Once the **dominant** member of our group makes up his mind about something, the rest of us go along with him.*

5. **durable** (dur' uh • bul) *adj.* Lasting; highly resistant to wear; capable of existing for a long time; not easily worn out.
   *My jeans are so **durable** that they will probably outlast me.*

6. **exceedingly** (ek • sēd' ing • lē) *adv.* Extremely.
   *José is **exceedingly** happy because he just won a scholarship to the college of his choice.*

7. **harmony** (har′ muh • nē) *n.* Agreement; getting along well together; accord; agreement of feelings, ideas, or actions. In music, the sounding together of two or more tones from a chord.

*In our community, there is so much disagreement among the elected officials that it seems impossible to achieve any **harmony** among them.*

8. **literally** (lit′ ur • ul • ē) *adv.* Word for word; in a strict sense; actually.

*After all the abuse that she took as a child, she **literally** went out of her mind.*

9. **prestige** (pres • tēzh′) *n.* High reputation or influence gained from success; the power to command respect, admiration, and so on from others; status.

*We couldn't believe that someone with such **prestige** would lend his name to a firm that has such a bad reputation.*

10. **status** (stāt′ us) *n.* The position of a person in relation to another or others; high standing; social standing; prestige.

*The protagonist in the play was always trying to improve her **status** in society by attempting to impress the wealthy people in her town.*

Practices

PRACTICE A

Directions: Choose a word from the word list that *best* fits the definition.

WORD LIST

compatible	discord	dogmatic	dominant	durable
exceedingly	harmony	literally	prestige	status

1. Extremely _____

2. Agreement _____

3. Disagreement _____

4. Lasting _____

5. Word for word _____

6. The power to command respect _____

7. The position of a person in relation to others _____

8. Ruling _____

9. Able to exist together _____

10. Exerting opinions as if they were fact _____

STOP. *Check answers at the back of the book on page 245.*

PRACTICE B

Directions: Choose a word from this lesson that *best* matches the meaning of the *italicized* word or words.

1. I feel that instructors should present information to students and that they should attempt to give both sides of an issue rather than be *opinionated*.

   _____

2. This semester there is so much *disagreement* among the students in my dormitory that I intend to live off campus next semester. _____

3. I like an environment in which there is *accord* rather than disagreement.

   _____

4. My roommate this semester is an *extremely* nice guy, but he has insomnia, so he never sleeps. _____

5. This has *actually* been the worst living situation I have encountered in my college life. _____

6. We are not *getting along well together* because he keeps me up all night talking about his personal problems. _____

7. My roommate is very concerned about his *position in relation to others*.

   _____

8. He likes to be with people who have *the power to command respect*.

   _____

9. I'm a pretty easy fellow to get along with and am not interested in exerting power over anyone; my roommate, however, is a *controlling* person.

   _____

10. It's easy to see why my friendship with my roommate could not be a *lasting* one. _____

> **STOP.** *Check answers at the back of the book on page 245.*

PRACTICE C

Directions: Choose the word from the word list that *best* fits in the blank. A word may be used once only. If necessary, you may change the form of the word in the word list.

WORD LIST

compatible	discord	dogmatic	dominant	durable
exceedingly	harmony	literally	prestige	status

It seems that Maria and Dave are very (1)_____. We expect that theirs is a(n) (2)_____ relationship that may result in marriage. They are (3)_____ happy together. It is interesting that Dave is not concerned that Maria earns more money than he does. He said that he does not need the (4)_____ that comes from earning more than his significant other, and this difference in income does not make either one of them the (5)_____ person in their relationship. They respect each other's opinions, and neither states an opinion in a(n) (6)_____ manner. It's safe to say that they are (7)_____ soulmates, and I have never seen any (8)_____ between them. Jim, however, says that Maria and Dave do not live in a state of (9)_____. He claims that he has seen them having a fight. It is more likely that Jim is jealous of Maria and Dave's relationship. Jim feels that he will gain (10)_____ among his friends by badmouthing Maria and Dave.

Multiple-Choice Assessment of Lessons 13–15

Directions: Words are arranged by lesson. Underline the meaning that *best* fits the word. Answers are at the back of the book. **If you miss any word meaning, go back to the lesson and restudy the word.**

LESSON 13

1. anticipate
   a. to pray for
   b. to be able to see
   c. to expect
   d. to look at in advance

2. astute
   a. stout
   b. clever
   c. always correct
   d. showy

3. charisma
   a. a strange power
   b. power used for evil
   c. a special gift
   d. personal charm used to inspire others

4. cope
   a. to try
   b. to deal with
   c. to struggle
   d. to avoid problems

5. duration
   a. a brief time period
   b. persistence
   c. everlasting time
   d. continuance in time

6. idealist
   a. perfect
   b. one who conforms to perfection
   c. one who conforms to most things
   d. one who conforms to life

7. **motivate**
   a. to be active
   b. to give power to
   c. to make angry
   d. to stimulate to action

8. **reality**
   a. the state of doing
   b. what actually exists
   c. what is practical
   d. what is impossible

9. **skeptical**
   a. inclined to doubt
   b. unquestioning
   c. not believing easily
   d. concerned with truth

10. **tedious**
    a. a tired person
    b. hard work
    c. boring
    d. continuing

LESSON 14

11. **citation**
    a. a saying
    b. a quotation
    c. a wise saying
    d. important writings

12. **cognitive**
    a. having to do with thinking
    b. working
    c. broad
    d. having to do with ideas

13. **comprehensive**
    a. referring to an exam
    b. referring to insurance
    c. of large scope
    d. understanding

14. **concept**
    a. writing
    b. thinking
    c. quotation
    d. idea

15. **objective**
    a. biased
    b. goal
    c. belonging to
       the mind
    d. mental things

16. **paraphrase**
    a. taking the writings of another
       as one's own
    b. a rewording of the writings
       of another
    c. repeating the writings of another
    d. using someone's work

17. **plagiarism**
    a. a liar
    b. the rewriting of something
    c. the act of taking the writings
       of another as one's own
    d. a leader for a cause

18. **protagonist**
    a. a fighter
    b. a novelist
    c. the main character
    d. a person of worth

19. **subjective**
    a. existing in the mind
    b. a brief statement
    c. unbiased
    d. a test

20. **synopsis**
    a. a restatement
    b. a quotation
    c. a brief statement
    d. a summary of a passage

LESSON 15

21. compatible
   a. capable
   b. able to live together
   c. able to survive
   d. living together

22. discord
   a. agreement
   b. opinions
   c. accord
   d. disagreement

23. dogmatic
   a. positive
   b. asserting opinions as fact
   c. negative
   d. differing opinions

24. dominant
   a. opinionated
   b. ruling
   c. agreement
   d. saying a lot

25. durable
   a. opinionated
   b. agreement
   c. lasting
   d. disagreement

26. exceedingly
   a. hardly
   b. extremely
   c. possibly
   d. trying

27. harmony
   a. disagreement
   b. opinionated
   c. agreement
   d. having to do with art

28. literally
   a. writing
   b. able to write
   c. able to read
   d. word for word

29. prestige
   a. a person's occupation
   b. power to command respect
   c. powerful
   d. a successful person

30. status
   a. success
   b. a powerful person
   c. social standing
   d. leadership

STOP. *Check answers at the back of the book on page 245.*

LESSON 16

adamant	amiable	amoral	avail	demoralize
disarray	emanate	extent	fetid	implore

1. **adamant** (ad′ uh • mant) *adj.* Unyielding; firm; immovable; stubborn.
   *Maria was **adamant** about her decision not to try out to be a cheerleader.*

2. **amiable** (ā′ me • uh • bul) *adj.* Good-natured; having a pleasant disposition; friendly.
   *Everyone likes to be around Erin because she is so **amiable** and easy to get along with.*

3. **amoral** (ā • mor′ ul) *adj.* Without a sense of right or wrong; without morals.
   *The jurors were trying to determine whether the woman who had murdered her children knew right from wrong or whether she was completely **amoral**.*

4. **avail** (uh • vāl′) *v.* To be of use, help, worth, or advantage. *n.* Effective use or help; advantage.
   *"I know I'm beginning to sound like my parents," Sandy said, "but if I want to improve my grades, it's to no **avail** to go out every night."*

5. **demoralize** (de • mor′ uh • līz) *n.* To lower the morale of; to weaken the spirit, courage, discipline of; to put into confusion.
   *Nothing could **demoralize** us more than to have the police take one of our buddies into custody for something he didn't do.*

6. **disarray** (dis • uh • rā′) *n.* Disorder; confusion; disordered or insufficient dress. *v.* To throw into disorder; to put into confusion.
   *The robbers left our room in such **disarray** that it took my roommate and me all day to straighten it out.*

7. **emanate** (em′ • uh • nāt) *v.* To come forth; to come out or proceed from a source; to give out.
   *The information that the water in our dorm room seemed to **emanate** from a pipe was not very helpful in identifying the leaking pipe.*

8. extent (ek • stent′) *n.* Length; area; volume or scope; the degree to which something extends; magnitude; range.

*Susan went to a great **extent** to convince us she was telling the truth, but the evidence against her was too strong.*

9. fetid (fet′ id) *adj.* Stinking; having a heavy offensive smell; smelling very bad.

*On hot days, you can smell the **fetid** swamp on the outskirts of town all over campus.*

10. implore (im • plor′) *v.* To beg or plead for earnestly or urgently.

*When Kevin was in the hospital, he **implored** the nurse to give him something stronger for the pain, but the nurse wouldn't do so without his doctor's approval.*

Practices

PRACTICE A

Directions: Choose a word from the word list that *best* fits the definition.

WORD LIST

adamant	amiable	amoral	avail	demoralize
disarray	emanate	extent	fetid	implore

1. Stubborn _____

2. Stinking _____

3. Confusion _____

4. Not knowing right from wrong _____

5. To beg urgently _____

6. Friendly _____

7. Length _____

8. To lower the morale of _____

9. To come from _____

10. To be of help _____

STOP. *Check answers at the back of the book on page 245.*

PRACTICE B

Directions: Choose a word from this lesson that *best* fits the blank in each sentence.

1. The parents of the kidnapped child went on television to _____ the kidnappers to return their child unharmed.

2. The chemicals gave off an exceedingly _____ odor.

3. Everything was in such a state of _____ after the hurricane struck our college town that it took us months to clean up, repair the damage, and get back to normal.

4. Our instructor was _____ about having the final exam on the scheduled day.

5. Many students tried to determine where the horrible smell in the dorm did _____ from.

6. They tried to _____ themselves of as much information about the dorm as they could.

7. Jane is the most _____ person in our dorm; everyone likes her because of her pleasant manner.

8. When the escaped prisoners took us hostage, they informed the police that they intended to _____ us into giving up hope.

9. The police did not know to what _____ the criminals would go to get what they wanted.

10. Some people wondered whether it was right to give into the criminals, and others said that it was ridiculous to try to bargain with people who seemed to be completely _____.

STOP. *Check answers at the back of the book on page 245.*

PRACTICE C

Directions: Choose the word from the word list that *best* fits in the blank. A word may be used once only. If necessary, you may change the form of the word.

WORD LIST

adamant	amiable	amoral	avail	demoralize
disarray	emanate	extent	fetid	implore

1. My friends were _____ about not going to the fraternity party.

2. To what _____ will you go ignoring Bill?

3. Patty must be _____ to have behaved in such an evil way.

4. I could not stand the _____ smell of the pond.

5. How _____ she is; no wonder so many people like to be around her.

6. To no _____ will you be able to talk me into going.

7. Her sorority sisters tried to _____ Erin to go to the party with them, telling her she needed a break from studying.

8. The bad gossip about Eric seemed to _____ from the person running against him in the election.

9. Eric said that he would not let anyone _____ him into giving up his candidacy for student council president.

10. Eric's campaign fell into a state of _____ when the vicious gossip about him first came out.

17

WORDS

absolve	animosity	eccentric	encounter	epitome
extant	malign	meticulous	rancid	saturated

1. absolve (ub • zalv′) *v.* To announce free from guilt or blame; to acquit; to free from.

*We told Megan that we would **absolve** her from her earlier commitment, which she made before she knew what was expected from her.*

2. animosity (an • uh • mos′ uh • tē) *n.* Hatred; resentment.

*She felt great **animosity** toward her roommates when they falsely accused her of copying from them.*

3. eccentric (uk • sen′ trik) *adj.* Deviating from the norm; out of the ordinary. *n.* An odd or unconventional person.

*At school many students thought that Mike was **eccentric** because he was always doing odd things.*

4. encounter (en • koun′ tur) *v.* To meet; to meet by chance; to come face to face with; to meet as an enemy. *n.* A meeting; a chance meeting; a meeting between enemies.

*Melissa said that the **encounter** with her former classmates was not too pleasant.*

5. epitome (ē • pit′ uh • mē) *n.* A person or thing that shows he or she has the typical qualities of something; a short statement of the main points of a report, book, or incident.

*Sara is the **epitome** of what I expect a responsible young person to be.*

6. extant (eks′ tunt) *adj.* Still existing; not lost or destroyed.

*Our dormitory is **extant**, but many of the others were destroyed in the fire that swept our campus.*

7. **malign** (muh • līn′) *v.* To speak ill or badly of; to slander.
*The politician said that he would not **malign** the person running against him, but he slandered him anyway.*

8. **meticulous** (muh • tik′ ū • lus) *adj.* Extremely careful and precise; extremely careful about details.
*We knew that something was amiss when we saw how disheveled Erin looked because normally she is so **meticulous** about her appearance that not one hair is out of place.*

9. **rancid** (ran′ sid) *adj.* Stale; spoiled; having an unpleasant, stale smell or taste; fetid.
*When the children used the word **rancid** to describe children, rather than food, we knew that they did not adequately understand the term.*

10. **saturated** (sach′ uh • rāt • id) *adj.* Full; soaked thoroughly; wet.
*Miriam was so **saturated** from the rain that she thought she would never dry out.*

Practices

PRACTICE A

Directions: Match the meaning with the word from the word list.

WORD LIST

absolve	animosity	eccentric	encounter	epitome
extant	malign	meticulous	rancid	saturated

1. Soaked thoroughly _____

2. Spoiled _____

3. Still existing _____

4. Extremely careful and precise _____

5. To meet by chance _____

6. To speak ill of _____

7. Out of the ordinary _____

8. Hatred _____

9. To announce free from guilt _____

10. Someone who typifies a trait or thing _____

STOP. *Check answers at the back of the book on page 245.*

PRACTICE B

Directions: Choose a word from the word list that *best* fits the blank in each sentence.

WORD LIST

absolve	animosity	eccentric	encounter	epitome
extant	malign	meticulous	rancid	saturated

1. It's not healthy to eat food that is _____ with fat.

2. Kim is the _____ of what I feel an ambitious young woman should be.

3. If butter or other food is left out too long without refrigeration, it will usually become _____.

4. The parents of the kidnapped child said that they would _____ the kidnapper of all guilt if only their child was returned unharmed.

5. Something that was well-built many years ago can be _____ today.

6. When we lost the race because Jim didn't come to practice as he should have, some team members felt great _____ toward him.

7. But others felt that it was unfair to _____ Jim when our team didn't win the race, especially since he had a good excuse for why he missed practice.

8. Most of us think that it's wrong to poke fun at someone who is _____ or has an unusual way of doing things.

9. I wasn't prepared to _____ one of my rivals at the race.

10. Joshua is very _____ about his appearance.

STOP. *Check answers at the back of the book on page 245.*

PRACTICE C

Directions: Choose the word from the word list that *best* fits in the blank. A word may be used once only. If necessary you may change the form of the word in the word list.

WORD LIST

absolve	animosity	eccentric	encounter	epitome
extant	malign	meticulous	rancid	saturated

1. The _____ between Melissa and Dave was a coincidence.

2. Rob is a(n) _____ who always seems to be doing strange things.

3. It was confusing when Anna said she had great _____ toward her boss when she meant just the opposite and actually liked him a lot.

4. The judge said that she could not _____ him of his guilt, but she would try to understand why he did what he did.

5. That tennis player is the _____ of the athlete I would like to be.

6. The _____ food smelled fetid.

7. If dinosaurs were _____ today, we probably would live in constant fear.

8. It would be a mismatch to have a sloppy person share a room with someone who is _____.

9. It rained so much yesterday that the ground was _____.

10. I hate it when politicians _____ one another in an effort to make themselves look better.

LESSON 18

WORDS

assess	constituent	deviate	espouse	heresy
lethargy	rampant	survey	vulnerable	wane

1. **assess** (uh • ses′) *v.* To estimate the value of property, income and so on for tax purposes; to fix or determine the amount of a tax, damages, a fine, and so on; to impose a tax on; to evaluate; to estimate the value or merit of something.
   *At many colleges, it's usual to **assess** each student a fee to support the student government.*

2. **constituent** (kun • stich′ ū • ent) *n.* Someone represented by another; client; a voter; one who elects or assists in electing another as his or her representative. *adj.* Forming a necessary part; serving as part of a whole; component.
   *The congressman said that he had to vote against the bill because he had promised every **constituent** in his district that he would do so.*

3. **deviate** (dē′ vē • āt) *v.* To turn aside or wander from the right or common path; to turn aside from a course, truth, line, way, and so on; to differ from the norm. (dē′ və • it) *n.* A person whose moral and social standards differ from the norm or from the usually accepted moral and social standards.
   *We decided to **deviate** from our usual routine, so we went dancing rather than bowling.*

4. **espouse** (uh • spouz′) *v.* To adopt or support some cause, view, and so on; to advocate; to give one's loyalty to and support to; to make one's own.
   *The cause that Bill believed in and that he tried to get us to **espouse** is not a very popular one, but that didn't stop Bill from supporting it.*

5. **heresy** (her′ uh • sē) *n.* An opinion or doctrine not in agreement with accepted doctrine; any belief or theory that varies strongly from accepted or established beliefs, customs, and so on.
   *In the Middle Ages, many people were tried for **heresy** because their religious views deviated from those of the Church.*

6. lethargy (leth′ ur • jē) *n*. The state and quality of being drowsy and dull; sluggish, inactivity; apathy.

*Although Fred had once climbed the highest mountain range in the world, when he returned, he dramatically changed, staying in bed all day and sinking into a deep state of **lethargy**.*

7. rampant (ram′ pant) *adj*. Growing without any check; wide-spreading; raging; angry; excited; violent inaction or spirit.

*In the monster film, the animals and plants exposed to the meteor were growing **rampant**, threatening to take over the world.*

8. survey (sur • vā′) *v*. To take a broad, general, or comprehensive view of; to look at, consider, or view as a whole; to determine the area, boundaries, or elevations of land by means of measuring angles and distances. (sur′ vā) *n*. A general or comprehensive view; a sampling or partial collection of opinions, fact, or figures taken and used to make an approximation of what a complete collection would be; a formal or official inspection or examination of the particulars of something to determine conditions, values, and so on.

*The political science instructor asked his students to help him **survey** people's opinions about the candidates in the upcoming election.*

9. vulnerable (vul′ ner • uh • bul) *adj*. Unprotected from danger; capable of being hurt; open to attack, criticism, temptation, and so on.

*We all have a weak spot that makes us **vulnerable** to attack by our enemies.*

10. wane (wān) *v*. To decrease gradually in size, amount, intensity, or degree; to decline. *n*. A gradual declining; growing less.

*Thanks to new medications and treatments, many diseases are on the **wane**.*

Practices

PRACTICE A

Directions: Match the word with the meaning that *best* fits.

Words	Meanings
_____ 1. lethargy	a. a voter
_____ 2. wane	b. an opinion not in agreement with accepted doctrine
_____ 3. constituent	c. unprotected from danger
_____ 4. espouse	d. sluggish inactivity
_____ 5. assess	e. wide-spreading
_____ 6. heresy	f. a sampling
_____ 7. deviate	g. evaluate
_____ 8. survey	h. to differ from the norm

_____ 9. rampant   i. to adopt or support some cause

_____ 10. vulnerable   j. to decline

STOP. *Check answers at the back of the book on page 245.*

PRACTICE B

Directions: Define the *italicized* word or words in each sentence.

1. I hoped I would not appear *vulnerable* in front of my former schoolmates.

   _____

2. Before an election, politicians often court their *constituents* with promises of extra funding for the school district. _____

3. Once I make up my mind to follow a certain path, it is difficult for me to *deviate* from it. _____

4. & 5. Galileo was tried for *heresy* because he *espoused* the view that the sun, not the earth, was the center of the universe. _____;

   _____

6. After I flunked a few exams, I decided to *assess* my study habits. _____

7. We knew that there was trouble in their relationship because Megan's feeling for Bob was on the rise, whereas Bob's feeling for Megan was on the *wane*.

   _____

8. The *rampant* growth of the plants in our backyard has dwarfed our house and made it seem as though we live in a jungle. _____

9. My friend became very *lethargic* after she lost lots of weight. _____

10. A *survey* of how people will vote was taken before the election.

    _____

STOP. *Check answers at the back of the book on page 245.*

PRACTICE C

Directions: Choose the word from the word list that *best* fits in the blank. A word may be used once only. If necessary, you may change the form of the word.

WORD LIST

assess	constituent	deviate	espouse	heresy
lethargy	rampant	survey	vulnerable	wane

1. Whenever politicians _____ their views, I wonder if the cause they are supporting is actually their own.

2. Politicians are usually out to get what they can for their _____.

3. They generally try to _____ who votes for them.

4. Before an election, politicians have opinion polls that _____ what the voters are interested in.

5. Politicians try to determine the most _____ voters so they can target their message to attract them.

6. Politicians usually vote with their leaders and do not _____ from their party's platform.

7. The party leadership would consider it almost _____ to vote with the other party.

8. It's funny to see some politicians during roll call because they appear to be in a state of _____.

9. Now with television homing in on those who doze off during roll call or speeches, the number of congresspeople falling asleep is on the _____.

10. Before television, however, the practice of falling asleep in chambers was _____.

Multiple-Choice Assessment of Lessons 16–18

Directions: Words are arranged by lesson. Underline the meaning that *best* fits the word. Answers are at the back of the book. **If you miss any word meaning, go back to the lesson and restudy the word.**

LESSON 16

1. adamant
  a. stubborn
  b. referring to fault
  c. yielding
  d. fresh

2. amiable
  a. not liked
  b. length
  c. friendly
  d. stubborn

3. amoral
  a. a right person
  b. not knowing right from wrong
  c. justice
  d. seeking revenge

4. avail
  a. stubborn
  b. to help
  c. referring to a veil
  d. to put off

5. demoralize
   a. justice
   b. not knowing right from wrong
   c. to seek justice
   d. to lower the morale of

6. disarray
   a. stubborn
   b. to come from
   c. confusion
   d. stinking

7. emanate
   a. to come from
   b. to make
   c. to go
   d. to smell

8. extent
   a. existing
   b. smell
   c. length
   d. stubborn

9. fetid
   a. friendly
   b. stubborn
   c. stinking
   d. smell

10. implore
   a. to come from
   b. to beg
   c. to pour
   d. to seek

LESSON 17

11. absolve
   a. to solve
   b. to acquit
   c. to find friendly
   d. to find guilty

12. animosity
   a. hatred
   b. full of spirit
   c. friendly
   d. full of hope

13. eccentric
   a. powerful
   b. odd
   c. unfriendly
   d. stubborn

14. encounter
   a. a chance meeting
   b. a friendly meeting
   c. share
   d. a powerful meeting

15. epitome
   a. the highest point
   b. a proper person
   c. typical of something
   d. a likable person

16. extant
   a. length
   b. broad
   c. present time
   d. presently existing

17. malign
   a. ill feeling
   b. to be sick
   c. to slander
   d. to hurt physically

18. meticulous
   a. safe
   b. extremely careful
   c. careless
   d. extremely careless

19. rancid
   a. spoiled
   b. stinking
   c. tasty
   d. refers to food

20. saturated
   a. filled with
   b. raining
   c. extremely dry
   d. tired

LESSON 18

21. assess
- a. praise
- b. add
- c. figure out
- d. evaluate

22. constituent
- a. a leader
- b. a person running for office
- c. someone represented by another
- d. a member of congress

23. deviate
- a. at the norm
- b. to roam
- c. to change
- d. to wander from what is right

24. espouse
- a. a husband or wife
- b. to be married
- c. a spouse
- d. to advocate

25. heresy
- a. an opinion
- b. an opinion not in agreement with established ones
- c. a favorable opinion
- d. an established opinion

26. lethargy
- a. without sleep
- b. sluggish inactivity
- c. fearful
- d. restless state

27. rampant
- a. a long path
- b. able to be checked
- c. wide-spreading
- d. useless

28. survey
- a. to vote
- b. to grow
- c. to help
- d. to examine for a purpose

29. vulnerable
- a. protected from danger
- b. capable of being hurt
- c. difficult to get to
- d. ready to hurt

30. wane
- a. to decline
- b. referring to the moon
- c. to increase
- d. shedding light

STOP. *Check answers at the back of the book on page 245.*

19

WORDS

apathy	beguile	caustic	empathy	equanimity
feign	intrigue	livid	opponent	taciturn

1. apathy (ap′ uh • thē) *n.* Lack of feeling; indifference.

*We couldn't believe that our instructor could have such **apathy** toward the failing student, but Mr. Evers said that because the student didn't care whether he flunked, neither did he.*

2. beguile (buh • gīl′) *v.* To deceive; to influence by deceit; to cheat; to charm or wile away pleasantly.

*At the amusement park, we were **beguiled** by all the people selling their wares, the rides, and other attractions.*

3. caustic (kos′ tik) *adj.* Able to burn, eat away, or dissolve by chemical action; cutting; stinging; biting; sarcastic.

*Pat's **caustic** remarks made everyone realize that she was still very angry with us.*

4. empathy (em′ puh • thē) *n.* Imagining oneself into the personality of another; ability to understand how another feels because one has experienced it firsthand or otherwise.

*Our roommate said she has great **empathy** for Jason because she has also broken her finger.*

5. equanimity (ek • wuh • nim′ uh • tē) *n.* Composure; the quality of being calm or even tempered; evenness of mind; balance.

*Even when under lots of stress, our instructor always seems to maintain his **equanimity**.*

6. feign (fān) *v.* To pretend; to make believe; to put on a false appearance of; to represent falsely; to invent.

*Melba always **feigned** ignorance whenever anyone asked her a question about her friend's background because she wanted to protect him.*

7. intrigue (in • trēg′) *n.* A secret or underhanded scheme; a secret love affair.
*In our dormitory, it seemed as though there was always some **intrigue** going on.*

8. livid (liv′ id) *adj.* Extremely angry; furious; discolored by bruising; ashen; pale.
*When Stacy heard how she had been tricked, she was **livid**.*

9. opponent (uh • pō′ nent) *n.* One who opposes another, as in battle or debate; an adversary or antagonist.
*My **opponent** in the debate has an excellent vocabulary.*

10. taciturn (tas′ uh • turn) *adj.* Untalkative; uncommunicative; inclined to silence.
*Everyone was very surprised when my usually **taciturn** roommate said that she would make a speech in honor of the occasion.*

Practices

PRACTICE A

Directions: Choose the word from the word list that *best* matches the meaning of the *italicized* word or phrase in each sentence.

WORD LIST

apathy	beguile	caustic	empathy	equanimity
feign	intrigue	livid	opponent	taciturn

1. Although not technically a strike, a sickout has the force of a strike, so on a specified day, the workers agreed to *pretend* illness and stay home from work.

   _____

2. We were surprised when the usually *untalkative* person tried to get his views across to the crowd. _____

3. Jack was really *furious* when he learned what his supposed best friend had said about him. _____

4. The chairperson's *composure* was broken when the server dropped the whole tray of food on the honored guest. _____

5. Most of us try hard to stay out of Ray's way because he has a sharp tongue, and his *biting* remarks stay with you for a long time. _____

6. Jessica tried to *deceive* him into thinking that she was in love with him.

   _____

7. We were shocked when we learned about the *underhanded scheme* our company was involved in to get a certain contract from the government. _____ _____

8. It was obvious by Kelly's behavior that she had complete *indifference* about how Ken felt toward her. _____

9. When Jim broke his leg skiing, Beth said that she had *experienced the same thing* a year ago, so she *knew how he felt* when it happened to him. _____ _____

10. My *adversary* in the debate is really a good speaker. _____

> **STOP.** *Check answers at the end of the book on page 246.*

PRACTICE B

Directions: Define the following words.

1. Apathy _____

2. Beguile _____

3. Caustic _____

4. Empathy _____

5. Equanimity _____

6. Feign _____

7. Intrigue _____

8. Livid _____

9. Opponent _____

10. Taciturn _____

> **STOP.** *Check answers at the back of the book on page 246.*

PRACTICE C

Directions: Choose the word from the word list that *best* fits the blank in each sentence. A word may be used once only. If necessary, you may also change the form of the word.

WORD LIST

apathy	beguile	caustic	empathy	equanimity
feign	intrigue	livid	opponent	taciturn

1. Last year my roommate did not seem to care much about anything; she showed _____ toward her school work.

2. Though we were not fooled, she used to _____ that she was a famous person in disguise.

3. She made _____ comments and was mean to my friends.

4. Even though I am usually pretty composed, it was hard for me to keep my _____ when I was in her presence.

5. Her unpleasant behavior made it easier for those who had never liked her to turn others against her, and soon everyone in the dorm was her _____. _____.

6. I learned that the best way to deal with her was to bite my tongue and be _____ in her presence, hardly saying anything to her.

7. When I learned more about her background, I felt kind of sorry for her, but her mean behavior made me feel little _____ for her.

8. She tried to stir up _____ among other girls in the dorm by spreading rumors.

9. But when she tried to _____ away my boyfriend with her stories, that was it for me.

10. I was completely _____ at her deceit and asked to be transferred to another dorm room.

LESSON 20

WORDS

crafty	derisive	ecstasy	listless	peruse
temerity	tenet	tentative	tenure	terminate

1. **crafty** (kraf' tē) *adj.* Sly; skillful in deceiving; cunning.
   *It's hard to trust people who are known to be sly or **crafty**.*

2. **derisive** (di • ri' siv) *adj.* Mocking, jeering.
   *Because some members of the class broke out into **derisive** laughter when other students spoke, I did not want to say anything.*

3. **ecstasy** (ek' stuh • sē) *n.* Great joy.
   *He was in a state of **ecstasy** when the love of his life consented to marry him.*

4. **listless** (list' less) *adj.* Lethargic; indifferent; inactive; apathetic; spiritless.
   *When the Smiths saw that their usually energetic child behaved in a lethargic and **listless** way, they took him to the doctor.*

5. **peruse** (puh • rūz') *v.* To read carefully; to inspect closely.
   *When I get an exam, I always **peruse** the directions very carefully so I know what is expected.*

6. **temerity** (tuh • mer' ut • ē) *n.* Rash boldness; foolhardiness.
   *I couldn't believe the **temerity** of the driver who passed five cars on a curve on a two-lane road.*

7. **tenet** (ten' ut) *n.* Belief; any opinion, doctrine, principle, dogma, and the like held as true.
   *Our instructor told us that the basic **tenet** for success in life is working hard.*

8. **tentative** (ten' tuh • tiv) *adj.* Uncertain; not final; done on trial or experimentally.
   *We made only **tentative** arrangements to meet in a year, because we really didn't know where we would be at that time.*

9. **tenure** (ten′ yūr) *n.* The right to hold or possess something; length of time something is held; status assuring an employee of permanence in his or her position or employment.

   *After a teacher receives **tenure**, it is often difficult to dismiss the person.*

10. **terminate** (tur′ muh • nāt) *v.* To end.

    *Our college decided to **terminate** the food service company because so many students complained about the poor service and food.*

SHOE reprinted by permission of Tribune Media Services.

Practices

PRACTICE A

Directions: Match the word with the meaning that *best* fits.

	Words	*Meanings*
_____	1. tenure	a. mocking
_____	2. tenet	b. sly
_____	3. temerity	c. belief
_____	4. crafty	d. rash boldness
_____	5. derisive	e. to end
_____	6. ecstasy	f. uncertain

_____ 7. listless   g. length of time something is held

_____ 8. peruse   h. great joy

_____ 9. terminate   i. to inspect carefully

_____ 10. tentative   j. lethargic

> **STOP.** _Check answers at the back of the book on page 246._

PRACTICE B

Directions: Choose a word from the word list that _best_ fits the blank in each sentence.

WORD LIST

crafty	derisive	ecstasy	listless	peruse
temerity	tenet	tentative	tenure	terminate

1. Kelsey had feelings of _____ when she heard that she had won the music prize.

2. We can only make _____ plans for a reunion because many of us do not know what we will be doing next year.

3. What _____ that reporter has to ask such questions of the victim!

4. I have a basic _____ for success that I try to follow.

5. We will have to _____ our plans for a fencing team next year because of the budget cuts.

6. The instructor was excited when he learned that he had received _____ _____ on his job.

7. That _____ man had all of us fooled when he presented his money-making scheme to us.

8. We were upset by the visiting actor's _____ remarks about the size of our school's theater.

9. My buddy developed an illness in his last year at school that made him very _____ and lethargic.

10. I always _____ my notes before an exam.

> **STOP.** _Check answers at the back of the book on page 246._

PRACTICE C

Directions: Choose the word from the word list that *best* fits in the blank. A word may be used once only. If necessary, you may also change the form of the word in the word list.

WORD LIST

| crafty | derisive | ecstasy | listless | peruse |
| temerity | tenet | tentative | tenure | terminate |

1. The plots of many television shows have to do with the characters' search for love and _____.

2. My friends and I _____ the TV schedule in the newspaper to find shows that deal with romance.

3. Some characters fall in love with someone they see from afar, but they quickly _____ their fervor for their object of affection.

4. Other characters are fairly _____ and shy about approaching their love interest.

5. Regardless of how much we like them, the _____ of some television shows is not very long.

6. If I watch too much TV, I start to feel tired and _____.

7. One of my friends, who has lots of _____, uses his _____ ways to get us to watch the shows he wants.

8. Another friend likes to watch shows where the actors insult each other with _____ comments and caustic putdowns.

9. My mother's basic _____ is that it's better to read than to watch TV.

LESSON 21

WORDS

alien	archetype	arrogant	bizarre	constraint
expedite	obfuscate	replenish	replete	thrifty

1. **alien** (ā′ lē • un) *n.* Foreigner; a person from another country; foreign.
   *After the attack on the World Trade Center, the immigration department cracked down on illegal **aliens**.*

2. **archetype** (ar′ ki • tīp) *n.* The original pattern or model.
   *We looked sadly at the **archetype** of the memorial to those who perished on September 11th.*

3. **arrogant** (ar′ uh • gunt) *adj.* Full of pride and self-importance; overbearing; haughty.
   *Some of the guys on the football team are **arrogant** and act like they own the school just because they are undefeated this year.*

4. **bizarre** (buh • zar′) *adj.* Very odd in manner, appearance, and so on; unexpected and unbelievable.
   *Our friend's sudden **bizarre** behavior really frightened us because we thought it might indicate he was having a nervous breakdown.*

5. **constraint** (kun • strānt′) *n.* Confinement; the act of restricting; the act of using force; compulsion; coercion; restriction.
   *One of the **constraints** of the job was that I couldn't leave whenever I desired.*

6. **expedite** (ek′ spuh • dīt) *v.* To hasten; to speed up the progress of.
   *The bookstore was out of the book I needed for class, so the salesman offered to **expedite** the book order so I could get it by the end of the week.*

7. **obfuscate** (ob • fus′ kāt) *v.* To darken; to confuse; to obscure.
   *Have you ever had an instructor who seemed to **obfuscate** rather than clarify information?*

8. replenish (ri • plen' ish) *v.* To supply or fill again.

*Unless the college bookstore was able to **replenish** its stock immediately, it would run out of supplies before the end of the semester.*

9. replete (ri • plēt') *adj.* Well-filled or supplied.

*It was obvious he admired his colleagues, because his words were **replete** with praise for them.*

10. thrifty (thrif' tē) *adj.* Clever at managing one's money; economical; not spending money unnecessarily.

*When you have a limited amount of money and lots of expenses, you have to be **thrifty**.*

Practices

PRACTICE A

Directions: Match the word with the meaning that *best* fits.

Words	*Meanings*
_____ 1. alien	a. to obscure
_____ 2. archetype	b. economically wise
_____ 3. arrogant	c. well-filled
_____ 4. bizarre	d. original model
_____ 5. constraint	e. haughty
_____ 6. expedite	f. restriction
_____ 7. obfuscate	g. odd
_____ 8. replenish	h. a foreigner
_____ 9. replete	i. to hasten
_____ 10. thrifty	j. to supply or fill again

STOP. *Check answers at the back of the book on page 246.*

PRACTICE B

Directions: Define the following words.

1. Alien _____

2. Archetype_____

3. Arrogant _____

4. Bizarre _____

5. Constraint _____

6. Expedite _____

7. Obfuscate _____

8. Replenish _____

9. Replete _____

10. Thrifty _____

> **STOP.** *Check answers at the end of the book on page 246.*

PRACTICE C

Directions: Choose the word from the word list that *best* fits the blank. A word may be used once only. If necessary, you may change the form of the word in the word list.

WORD LIST

alien	archetype	arrogant	bizarre	constraint
expedite	obfuscate	replenish	replete	thrifty

1. I dislike _____ people who act as though they are better than others.

2. Because I've always been quiet and shy, the idea of behaving as though I was superior to others would be _____ to me.

3. I have an instructor whose explanations seem to _____ the material rather than make it clear.

4. During the holidays, I have many gifts to buy but a limited amount of money, so I better be _____ .

5. I know it is _____, but I really do like to stay on campus when it is almost empty.

6. Our college snack shop is _____ with food to provide for those who remain on campus during the holidays.

7. It is important that I _____ the completion of all my assignments before I leave for holiday break.

8. Fortunately, the college bookstore has _____ its stock of books for next semester because I am going to get the ones I need for my courses now.

9. Having to stay on campus during the holiday break is one of the _____ _____ of going to a school that is so far away from my home.

10. We all admired the _____ of the building.

Multiple-Choice Assessment of Lessons 19–21

Directions: Words are arranged by lesson. Underline the meaning that *best* fits the word. Answers are at the back of the book. **If you miss any word meaning, go back to the lesson and restudy the word.**

LESSON 19

1. apathy
   a. full of feelings
   b. angry
   c. indifferent
   d. quiet

2. beguile
   a. desire
   b. amuse
   c. deceive
   d. help

3. caustic
   a. lye
   b. cheat
   c. able to burn
   d. deceive

4. empathy
   a. feeling
   b. strong feelings about something
   c. sympathy
   d. knowing how another feels

5. equanimity
   a. composure
   b. change
   c. pretend
   d. equal

6. feign
   a. believe
   b. creative
   c. pretend
   d. change

7. intrigue
   a. closed
   b. secret
   c. open
   d. underhanded scheme

8. livid
   a. refers to liver
   b. yells a lot
   c. fun-loving
   d. very angry

9. opponent
   a. opposite
   b. adversary
   c. someone who agrees
   d. debater

10. taciturn
   a. speaks a lot
   b. says little
   c. stutters when speaking
   d. doesn't like discussions

LESSON 20

11. crafty
a. silly
b. refers to crafts
c. good in the arts
d. sly

12. derisive
a. jeering
b. amicable
c. friendly
d. despise

13. ecstasy
a. great joy
b. refers to creativity
c. happy
d. exotic

14. listless
a. active
b. unhappy
c. apathetic
d. ill

15. peruse
a. look at
b. look at briefly
c. help
d. look at carefully

16. temerity
a. rashly bold
b. brave
c. bold
d. fearful

17. tenet
a. opinionated
b. refers to tents
c. belief
d. tense

18. tentative
a. for a long time
b. temporarily
c. briefly
d. in awhile

19. tenure
a. length of time
b. refers to ten
c. length of time something is held
d. held for awhile

20. terminate
a. remain
b. refers to termites
c. end
d. refers to terms

LESSON 21

21. alien
a. another country
b. an illegal person
c. a foreigner
d. a poor person

22. archetype
a. a new building
b. original model
c. a plan
d. an arch

23. arrogant
a. referring to anger
b. haughty
c. referring to poor
d. silly

24. bizarre
a. strange
b. busy
c. silly
d. poor

25. **constraint**
   a. refers to a rope
   b. restriction
   c. tension
   d. strain

26. **expedite**
   a. to hurry somewhere
   b. to hasten
   c. to speed in a car
   d. to progress

27. **obfuscate**
   a. to lighten
   b. to fuse
   c. to confuse
   d. to inform

28. **replenish**
   a. to supply again
   b. to plan well
   c. to help
   d. to apply again

29. **replete**
   a. to supply
   b. to keep
   c. well-filled
   d. well-ordered

30. **thrifty**
   a. wise
   b. witty
   c. economically wise
   d. sly

STOP. *Check answers at the back of the book on page 246.*

LESSON 22

awe	castigate	laudable	prudent	satiate
sedate	vindicate	vindictive	virile	vital

1. awe (aw) *n.* Respect tinged with fear; an overwhelming feeling of respect, fear, or admiration produced by someone or something powerful or the like.
*Everyone at school seemed to be in **awe** of the football players.*

2. castigate (kas′ ti • gāt) *v.* To correct or subdue by punishing; to criticize with drastic severity; to rebuke.
*The student council **castigated** the students who brought liquor into the dorm.*

3. laudable (lawd′ uh • bul) *adj.* Worthy of praise; commendable.
*Because not many students volunteered to give up their free time to help in the soup kitchen, it's **laudable** that Dave and his friends did.*

4. prudent (prū′ dent) *adj.* Not rash; wisely cautious; sensible; capable of using sound judgment in practical matters.
*Carol and Sharon are always **prudent** in dealing with money matters.*

5. satiate (sā′ shē • āt) *v.* To fill; to satisfy the appetite completely; to supply with anything to excess; to glut oroverindulge.
*There was so much food that even the members of the football team were able to **satiate** their appetites at the party.*

6. sedate (suh • dāt′) *v.* To calm; to put under sedation. *adj.* Calm; composed; quiet; serene; sober.
*After Mike took a tranquilizer, he became very **sedate**.*

7. vindicate (vin′ duh • kāt) *v.* To clear from criticism, accusation, or suspicion.
*Although our friend was completely **vindicated** by the trial, some people still treated her as if she were guilty.*

8. **vindictive** (vin • dik′ tiv) *adj.* Spiteful; revengeful in spirit.

*It's difficult not to be **vindictive** toward those who have harmed members of your family.*

9. **virile** (vir′ ul) *adj.* Manly; masculine; forceful; able to procreate; to produce or reproduce.

***Virile** men do not have to prove their masculinity to anyone.*

10. **vital** (vī′ tul) *adj.* Necessary to life; essential; energetic.

*When we heard how **vital** the operation was, we tried to convince our friend to have it.*

"LET'S REMEMBER TO KEEP OUR MIND ON THE VITAL STATISTICS AND NOT THE FASCINATING ONES!"

NEA reprinted by permission of Newspaper Enterprise Association, Inc.

Practices

PRACTICE A

Directions: Match the meaning with the word from the word list.

WORD LIST

awe	castigate	laudable	prudent	satiate
sedate	vindicate	vindictive	virile	vital

1. Calm _____

2. Worthy of praise _____

3. Wise _____

4. To clear from criticism _____

5. To correct or subdue by punishing _____

6. Essential _____

7. To fill _____

8. Manly _____

9. Spiteful _____

10. Respect tinged with fear _____

STOP. *Check answers at the end of the book on page 246.*

PRACTICE B

Directions: Match the word with the meaning that *best* fits.

	Words	*Meanings*
_____	1. awe	a. necessary to life
_____	2. castigate	b. wise
_____	3. laudable	c. calm
_____	4. prudent	d. to clear from guilt
_____	5. satiate	e. worthy of praise
_____	6. sedate	f. manly
_____	7. vindicate	g. respect tinged with fear
_____	8. vindictive	h. to satisfy the appetite completely
_____	9. virile	i. to subdue by punishing
_____	10. vital	j. spiteful

STOP. *Check answers at the end of the chapter on page 246.*

PRACTICE C

Directions: Choose the word from the word list that *best* fills the blank. A word may be used once only. If necessary, you may change the form of the word in the word list.

WORD LIST

awe	castigate	laudable	prudent	satiate
sedate	vindicate	vindictive	virile	vital

1. Please do not _____ me for doing such a stupid thing.

2. At the party we needed a(n) _____ person to move some of the furniture.

3. I'm embarrassed to know that what I did was not _____.

4. Everyone at the party was in _____ of me when I ate and drank so much in the pig-out contest.

5. I know that it was not the _____ thing to do.

6. I was tired from pulling an all-nighter studying for a test, so I was in a _____ mood when I first arrived at the party.

7. The party was so dead that I felt it was _____ for me to liven it up.

8. After eating and drinking so much, I am _____.

9. Do you think that the dean will be _____ and decide to give me a harsh punishment when he finds out about the pig-out contest?

10. It is important to _____ everyone at the party who didn't participate in the contest.

WORDS

corroborate	criterion	datum/data	exonerate	invincible
jeopardy	repent	signify	temperate	valid

1. **corroborate** (kuh • rob′ uh • rāt) *v.* To confirm; to strengthen; to make firm; to affirm; to make more certain.
   *Selina **corroborated** our suspicions concerning Sam's guilt when she testified that Sam tried to sell Jim stolen goods.*

2. **criterion** (krī • tir′ ē • un) *n.* (pl. **criteria**) (krī • tir′ ē • uh) In the singular—A standard of judging; any established rule, law, or principle by which a correct judgment can be made.
   *Our instructor told us the **criteria** that she would use to evaluate our essays.*

3. **datum** (dā • tum′) *n.* (pl. **data**) (dā • tuh′) (Usually used in the plural.) Information given; a premise upon which something can be argued; material that is often used as a basis for calculations. (At times, **data** is used for the singular.)
   *Because of insufficient **data**, we couldn't determine Mary Lou's guilt or innocence.*

4. **exonerate** (ig • zon′ uh • rāt) *v.* To clear of a charge of guilt; to prove blameless; to relieve of a debt or duty; to relieve of a charge or of blame resting on one.
   *We were overjoyed when our friend was **exonerated** of bringing illegal drinks to the party.*

5. **invincible** (in • vin′ suh • bul) *adj.* Impossible to overcome; not able to be conquered.
   *José bragged that his powerful serve made him **invincible** when he played tennis and that no one could beat him.*

6. **jeopardy** (jep′ ur • dē) *n.* Danger; risk; peril.
   *Dave knew that he was putting his life in **jeopardy** when he testified against the drug dealers on his block.*

7. **repent** (ri • pent′) *v.* To feel regret, pain, or sorrow for something left undone; to feel remorse.
   *Joe **repented** that he had not been kinder to his mother and father when they were alive.*

8. **signify** (sig′ nuh • fī) *v.* To be a sign of; to make known, as by signs, words, and so forth.
   *At the meeting, we were told to **signify** our approval by saying "Aye."*

9. **temperate** (tem′ per • it) *adj.* Moderate in everything one does; avoiding extremes or excesses.
   *My parents like my **temperate** boyfriend a lot because he never eats or drinks too much.*

10. **valid** (val′ id) *adj.* Having legal force; sound; well-grounded on principle or evidence; accurate.
   *The instructor decided that Jim's excuse for missing the test because he had a temperature of 102 was **valid**.*

Practices

PRACTICE A

Directions: Match the meaning with the word from the word list.

WORD LIST

corroborate	criterion	datum/data	exonerate	invincible
jeopardy	repent	signify	temperate	valid

1. To make known _____

2. Sound _____

3. Danger _____

4. Difficult to overcome _____

5. Affirm _____

6. Moderate _____

7. Feeling remorse _____

8. A standard for judging _____

9. Free from guilt _____

10. Facts often used for arguing a point _____

> **STOP.** *Check answers at the back of the book on page 246.*

PRACTICE B

Directions: Define the words below.

1. Corroborate _____

2. Criterion _____

3. Datum/data _____

4. Exonerate _____

5. Invincible _____

6. Jeopardy _____

7. Repent _____

8. Temperate _____

9. Signify _____

10. Valid _____

> **STOP.** *Check answers at the back of the book on page 246.*

PRACTICE C

Directions: Choose the word from the word list that *best* fits in the blank. A word may be used once only. If necessary, you may change the form of the word in the word list.

WORD LIST

corroborate	criterion	datum/data	exonerate	invincible
jeopardy	repent	signify	temperate	valid

1. In the movie, the protagonist, who was in prison, was always in _____ _____ of getting hurt.

2. He never _____ because he claimed that he was innocent of the crime.

3. No matter how poorly he was treated, his determination to get out of prison and clear his name remained _____.

4. His girlfriend tried everything she could think of to _____ him and prove his innocence.

5. She _____ to the prison warden what she was trying to do.

6. The warden told her that there had to be no doubt that her new information proving the prisoner's innocence was _____.

7. The warden said that the courts had set up very strict _____ for determining if a prisoner could get a new trial based on new evidence.

8. The lawyer _____ to the warden the girlfriend's beliefs about the new evidence.

9. The lawyer told her that she would have to maintain a(n) _____ manner in court to avoid seeming too emotional and to keep her credibility.

10. The girlfriend was successful in presenting the _____ in the new trial and was able to clear her boyfriend.

LESSON 24

WORDS

abridge	amend	apt	attrition	finite
futile	imminent	infinite	parse	phenomenon

1. **abridge** (uh • brij′) *v.* To shorten; to give the substance of in fewer words; to curtail.
   *The kindergarten teachers decided to **abridge** some of the longer stories so they would be more suitable for their young students' attention span.*

2. **amend** (uh • mend′) *v.* To make better; to improve; to change or revise; to correct.
   *The legislators said that the tax bill had to be **amended** because as it now stood, it wouldn't pass.*

3. **apt** (apt) *adj.* Appropriate; suited to its purpose; fitting; quick to learn or understand; tending or inclined toward.
   *We are more **apt** to want to study with the best student in the class than with the worst.*

4. **attrition** (uh • trish′ un) *n.* A gradual wearing down or weakening; a rubbing out or grinding down.
   *Rather than laying off employees, the owner of the company waited for people to quit, using a gradual **attrition** to trim her workforce.*

5. **finite** (fī′ nīt) *adj.* Having a limit or end; able to be measured.
   *Our dorm room is so small that when we lose something, there is only a **finite** number of places where it can be.*

6. **futile** (fū′ tul) *adj.* Useless; ineffectual; unimportant; trifling.
   *The paramedics realized that the man was already dead, so any efforts to revive him would be **futile**.*

7. **imminent** (im′ uh • nunt) *adj.* About to happen; threatening.
   *When the islanders heard that a hurricane was **imminent**, they boarded up their homes.*

8. **infinite** (in' fuh • nit) *adj.* Having no limit or end; not able to be measured.
   *There seem to be an **infinite** number of stars in the sky.*

9. **parse** (pars) *v.* Explaining the grammatical form and use of each of the parts of a sentence and their interrelationships; to separate a sentence into parts; to describe the form, use, and interrelationships of a word in a sentence.
   *Years ago, it was considered an important grammatical skill to be able to **parse** a sentence.*

10. **phenomenon** (fi • nom' uh • non) *n.* (pl. **phenomena** (fi • nom' uh • nuh) Any fact, circumstance, or experience that is apparent to the senses and that can be scientifically described; something extremely unusual.
    *The eclipse of the sun by the moon is a **phenomenon** that is easy for nonscientists to observe.*

SHOE reprinted by permission of Tribune Media Services.

Practices

PRACTICE A

Directions: Match the meaning with the word from the word list.

WORD LIST

abridge	amend	apt	attrition	finite
futile	imminent	infinite	parse	phenomenon

1. To separate a sentence into its grammatical parts _____

2. Change _____

3. Shorten _____

4. A wearing down _____

5. Never ending _____

6. Useless _____

7. Something that has an end _____

8. Something about to happen _____

9. Appropriate _____

10. Something extremely unusual _____

> **STOP.** *Check answers at the back of the book on page 246.*

PRACTICE B

Directions: Define the words below.

1. Abridge _____

2. Amend _____

3. Apt _____

4. Attrition _____

5. Finite _____

6. Futile _____

7. Imminent _____

8. Infinite _____

9. Parse _____

10. Phenomenon _____

> **STOP.** *Check answers at the back of the book on page 246.*

PRACTICE C

Directions: Choose the word from the word list that *best* fills the blank. A word may be used once only. If necessary, you may change the form of the word in the word list.

WORD LIST

abridge	amend	apt	attrition	finite
futile	imminent	infinite	parse	phenomenon

1. Have you read the _____ or complete version of that book?

2. In our English class, our instructor asked us to _____ the various parts of a sentence in the book we were reading.

3. Did you _____ your previous statement to make it sound more believable?

4. When Tanisha said that she had witnessed a UFO, most of us did not believe that she had seen the _____.

5. Tanisha loves science fiction; her favorite saying is, "To _____ and beyond!"

6. She claims there are more planets in our solar system than the _____ number now accepted.

7. She is quite _____ in discussing all aspects of the *Star Wars* and *Star Trek* movies.

8. She does not think it is a(n) _____ effort to try to contact UFOs.

9. Do you remember when Tanisha claimed a meteor crash was _____ and that it would destroy the earth?

10. The mother's resolve gradually collapsed under the _____ of her son's constant nagging for the new puppy

Multiple-Choice Assessment of Lessons 22–24

Directions: Words are arranged by lesson. Underline the meaning that best fits the word. Answers are at the end of the book. **If you miss any word meaning, go back to the lesson and restudy the word.**

LESSON 22

1. awe
a. to cry
b. hurtful
c. respect tinged with fear
d. caring

2. castigate
a. scream at
b. to hit
c. cry about
d. to rebuke

3. laudable
a. worthy
b. worthy of praise
c. a worthwhile cause
d. a worthwhile person

4. prudent
a. rashly bold
b. scared
c. rash
d. wise

5. satiate
   a. to satisfy the appetite of
   b. to restrict
   c. to fill again
   d. smug

6. sedate
   a. to help
   b. to give a needle to
   c. to calm
   d. to give drink to

7. vindicate
   a. to help
   b. to clear from suspicion
   c. to make guilty
   d. to become a victim

8. vindictive
   a. spiteful
   b. killing
   c. to hurt
   d. to clear from guilt

9. virile
   a. referring to being a sissy
   b. masculine
   c. referring to growing hair
   d. referring to love

10. vital
   a. referring to manly
   b. helpful
   c. necessary
   d. to calm

LESSON 23

11. corroborate
   a. to establish
   b. to make true
   c. to confirm
   d. to lie about

12. criterion
   a. a fact
   b. a truth
   c. a standard of judging
   d. a judgment

13. datum/data
   a. truth
   b. information used
   c. observed
   d. whatever is known

14. exonerate
   a. to prove blameless
   b. to prove friendly
   c. to prove guilty
   d. to disprove

15. invincible
   a. difficult
   b. easy to overcome
   c. difficult to overcome
   d. not able to be seen

16. jeopardy
   a. a game
   b. hurt
   c. danger
   d. fearful

17. repent
   a. refers to feelings
   b. refers to crying
   c. remorse
   d. tearful

18. signify
   a. to make known
   b. important
   c. refers to studies
   d. refers to research

19. temperate
a. moderate
b. eating well
c. calm
d. refers to temperature

20. valid
a. unnecessary information
b. refers to research
c. sound
d. refers to studies

LESSON 24

21. abridge
a. refers to length
b. to bridge
c. refers to children
d. to shorten

22. amend
a. to harm
b. to lengthen
c. to change
d. to shorten

23. apt
a. inappropriate
b. refers to some people
c. appropriate
d. refers to all people

24. attrition
a. refers to employers
b. the act of wearing down
c. refers to employees
d. the firing of employees

25. finite
a. no end
b. refers to the universe
c. having an end
d. refers to story endings

26. futile
a. useless
b. refers to death
c. useful
d. refers to an end

27. imminent
a. trying to hasten something
b. to make something happen
c. about to happen
d. a happening

28. infinite
a. having an end
b. something unusual
c. refers to the universe
d. never ending

29. parse
a. a part of speech
b. a parrot
c. a self-contradiction in a sentence
d. to explain a word in a sentence

30. phenomenon
a. something unusual
b. an eclipse
c. a happening
d. facts

STOP. *Check answers at the back of the book on page 246.*

WORDS

abstract	austere	celibacy	compensate	delve
deprecate	esoteric	improvise	query	redundant

1. **abstract** (ab′ strakt) *adj*. Not concrete; expressing a quality of thought apart from any material or particular object. *n*. A brief statement of the essential content of a book or article; a summary; an idea that is not concrete. (ab • strakt′) *v*. To summarize; to take away; remove.
   *Our instructor's mathematical theories are usually too **abstract** for us to understand, so we asked him to give us an **abstract** of his views.*

2. **austere** (aw • ster′) *adj*. Having a stern or severe look or manner; forbidding; very plain; lacking ornament or luxury; self-denial.
   *Because Dina's party dress was so **austere**, we suggested that she add some ornaments to it to make it look more festive.*

3. **celibacy** (sel′ uh • buh • sē) *n*. The state of being unmarried; complete sexual abstinence.
   *In the Catholic Church, priests vow never to marry and are supposed to practice **celibacy**.*

4. **compensate** (kom′ pun • sāt) *v*. To make up for; to make equivalent; to make amends for something.
   *When Bill lost Molly's bike, he said he would **compensate** her for what it was worth.*

5. **delve** (delv) *v*. To search; to investigate for information; to dig up or turn up.
   *Imagine our surprise to learn that the hosts of the weekend party had spent weeks trying to **delve** into our pasts so they could decide who to invite.*

6. **deprecate** (dep′ ruh • kāt) *v.* To feel and express disapproval of; to belittle.

   *My classmates and I felt that it was wrong and highly unprofessional for our instructor to **deprecate** another instructor in public.*

7. **esoteric** (es • uh • ter′ ik) *adj.* Understood by a select few; beyond the understanding of most people; hard to understand.

   *Bill devised such an **esoteric** theory, based on a combination of philosophy and science, for our group project on space exploration that we had a hard time understanding how to implement it.*

8. **improvise** (im′ pruh • vīs) *v.* To do on the spur of the moment; to do without any preparation; to bring about with whatever is at hand.

   *When our group had only an hour to prepare for our presentation, Dick said that we needed to **improvise** using the material we already had.*

9. **query** (kwer′ ē) *n.* A question; inquiry. *v.* To question.

   *After someone was killed on campus, the police had to **query** us all to find out if we knew the victim.*

10. **redundant** (ri • dun′ dunt) *adj.* More than enough; excess; unnecessary, especially in relation to word meaning.

    *Our instructor told us to use clear, concise language and avoid being **redundant** when writing our essays.*

Practices

PRACTICE A

Directions: Match the meaning with the word from the word list.

WORD LIST

abstract	austere	celibacy	compensate	delve
deprecate	esoteric	improvise	query	redundant

1. Belittle _____

2. Unnecessary _____

3. Question _____

4. Make up for _____

5. Known to only a few _____

6. Severe _____

7. Dig deeply _____

8. The state of being unmarried _____

9. To do without any preparation _____

10. Not concrete _____

STOP. *Check answers at the back of the book on page 247.*

PRACTICE B

Directions: Define the words below.

1. Abstract _____

2. Austere _____

3. Celibacy _____

4. Compensate _____

5. Delve _____

6. Deprecate _____

7. Esoteric _____

8. Improvise _____

9. Query _____

10. Redundant _____

STOP. *Check answers at the back of the book on page 247.*

PRACTICE C

Directions: Choose the word from the word list that *best* fits in the blank. A word may be used once only. If necessary, you may change the form of the word in the word list.

WORD LIST

abstract	austere	celibacy	compensate	delve
deprecate	esoteric	improvise	query	redundant

1. It seemed _____ to have written street directions as well as a map on our poster.

2. Please _____ more deeply into that matter until you get all the information.

3. Here is the _____ of the eight-day trial; I hope it helps you sum up the case.

4. In elections, it seems that the politicians _____ one another's characters.

5. At times some politicians obfuscate the issues and speak in _____ terms the average voter can't understand.

6. Lately, because of the scandals involving many Catholic priests, some people have said that the church leadership should discuss the _____ of priests.

7. It seems that perhaps the standards for Catholic priests in relation to marriage are too _____, and many have trouble sticking to these strict rules.

8. When people were _____ about the idea of priests in the Catholic Church marrying, most answered that they weren't sure if it was a good idea.

9. Some imaginative people can _____ and create something new from the materials they have at hand.

10. The blind man had a keen sense of hearing to help _____ for his loss of sight.

26

WORDS

dire	extrinsic	feasible	intrinsic	libel
morality	ominous	ornate	placid	pragmatic

1. **dire** (dīr) *adj.* Causing extreme distress; terrible; dreadful; extreme.
   *One of our friends caused the **dire** fire at our dorm because he had fallen asleep while holding a lit cigarette.*

2. **extrinsic** (eks • trin′ sik) *adj.* Not really belonging to the thing with which it is connected; coming from the outside.
   *Jim learned that many things he had valued before going away to school were really **extrinsic** to his basic needs and desires.*

3. **feasible** (fē′ zuh • bul) *adj.* Capable of being done; possible; within reason; practicable; probable; likely; capable of being used successfully; suitable.
   *Although Erin's plan was a complex one, it was still **feasible** for us to carry it out.*

4. **intrinsic** (in • trin′ sek) *adj.* Essential; belonging to the true nature of something; not dependent on the external particulars of something.
   *Jake is more concerned with the **intrinsic** value of something than with its superficial appearance.*

5. **libel** (lī′ bul) *n.* Any false or malicious writing or picture or whatever that attempts to defame a person and subject him or her to public ridicule, hatred, or contempt; an attempt to injure a person's reputation in some way. *v.* To try to injure a person's reputation in some way.
   *Jim said he had retained a lawyer and would sue for **libel** because his reputation was ruined by the magazine writer's lies in the article about his business dealings.*

6. **morality** (muh • ral′ i • tē) *n.* The character of being in accord with the principles or standards of right conduct; right conduct.
   Maria said that she always tried to do what she considered right because ***morality*** *meant a lot to her.*

7. **ominous** (om′ uh • nus) *adj.* Threatening; sinister; evil.
   The ***ominous*** *clouds warned us that it would probably rain and that we would have to reschedule our picnic.*

8. **ornate** (or • nāt′) *adj.* Showy; heavily adorned.
   We couldn't understand why our friend Sara liked to wear such ***ornate*** *clothes because she was not a showy person.*

9. **placid** (plas′ id) *adj.* Calm; quiet.
   Sara's choice of flashy clothes is surprising for such a ***placid*** *person.*

10. **pragmatic** (prag • mat′ ik) *adj.* Having to do with the practical aspects of everyday things rather than with theoretical speculation.
    We prided ourselves on being ***pragmatic*** *in our business dealings with others.*

Practices

PRACTICE A

Directions: Match the meaning with the word from the word list.

WORD LIST

dire	extrinsic	feasible	intrinsic	libel
morality	ominous	ornate	placid	pragmatic

1. Terrible _____

2. Practical _____

3. External _____

4. Internal _____

5. Threatening _____

6. Showy _____

7. Calm _____

8. False or malicious writing _____

9. Right conduct _____

10. Capable of being done _____

> **STOP.** *Check answers at the end of the book on page 247.*

PRACTICE B

Directions: Choose the word from the word list that *best* fits the blank in each sentence.

WORD LIST

dire	extrinsic	feasible	intrinsic	libel
morality	ominous	ornate	placid	pragmatic

1. Because Megan claims to have such a strong sense of _____, we couldn't believe that she had told those vicious lies about her supposed best friend, Lisa.

2. Fred said, however, that it was _____ Megan had said what she did, based on her behavior toward Lisa as of late.

3. We agreed, but we couldn't believe that Megan would resort to _____ to besmirch her friend.

4. We told Megan that she was behaving in a(n) _____ way.

5. It is hard to remain _____ in the midst of someone who we feared had told lies about another of our friends.

6. Also, because we saw both Megan and Lisa every day, it was hard to be _____, that is, practical rather than theoretical about what had occurred.

7. We also thought that it was odd that Megan began to wear such _____ clothes.

8. Megan hated to be showy, so we wondered why her _____ behavior was presently so different.

9. Lisa said that Megan was not herself; she said that even though Megan's external behavior had changed, her_____ behavior probably hadn't changed.

10. It was really an extremely _____ situation for all of us to see Megan changing before our eyes. We thought we knew her.

> **STOP.** *Check answers at the back of the book on page 247.*

PRACTICE C

Directions: Choose the word from the word list that *best* fits in the blank. A word may be used once only. If necessary, you may change the form of the word in the word list.

WORD LIST

dire	extrinsic	feasible	intrinsic	libel
morality	ominous	ornate	placid	pragmatic

1. & 2. The terms _____ and _____ contradict each other.

3. When I questioned the _____ of my roommate, Rosina, others at school told me I was being like an old woman.

4. Rosina would _____ another girl and talk about how she slept with everyone she met. How funny that Rosina saw in others what she didn't see in herself.

5. It's just not _____ for me to continue sharing a room with Rosina.

6. I don't like her behavior and feel strongly that she behaves in such a(n) _____ way because she has seen her parents behave in the same way.

7. Rosina likes to wear _____ clothes, and that is exactly how I feel her behavior is—showy.

8. Rosina appears to be a(n) _____ person on the outside, but she is anything but quiet.

9. I am a(n) _____ person, that is, if it is practical, I will go along with it, but Rosina's behavior is just too much for me.

10. I feel that Rosina will be in _____ trouble if she doesn't amend her ways.

WORDS

affinity	contemporary	convene	deference	didactic
eclectic	hypothesis	poignant	pretentious	ridicule

1. **affinity** (uh • fin′ uh • tē) *n.* Attraction to one another; close relationship.
   *When Kim and Herb met, they had such an **affinity** for one another that they knew their relationship would become something special.*

2. **contemporary** (kun • tem′ puh • rer • ē) *adj.* Modern; happening at the same time; of the same age.
   *At school, all my friends are my **contemporaries**.*

3. **convene** (kun • vēn′) *v.* To come together; assemble.
   *The student council said that it would **convene** its first meeting a week after classes began.*

4. **deference** (def′ ur • uns) *n.* Respect; a giving in to another's opinion or judgment.
   *At the meeting, everyone was very polite, and in **deference** to Mr. Palsey's age and position, the students let him speak first.*

5. **didactic** (dī • dak′ tik) *adj.* Related to instruction and teaching; at times may be overly concerned with teaching.
   *Many of our instructors try to present **didactic** lessons that teach us something.*

6. **eclectic** (ek • lek′ tik) *adj.* Made up of numerous things; selecting from various sources.
   *Our instructor told us at the beginning of the semester that he was an **eclectic** person who believed in pulling material from many different sources.*

7. **hypothesis** (hī • poth′ uh • sis) *n.* An unproved scientific conclusion drawn from known facts; a possible answer to a problem that requires further investigation.

   *The **hypothesis** put forth as the answer to the problem seemed logical, but it required further investigation to determine whether it was correct.*

8. **poignant** (poin′ yunt) *adj.* Emotionally moving; arousing pity.

   *The scene when the heroine finds that her lover has committed suicide is a very **poignant** one.*

9. **pretentious** (prē • ten′ shus) *adj.* Making claims that one is important; showy.

   *I would never choose a person to be a friend if he or she were to behave in a **pretentious** manner.*

10. **ridicule** (rid′ uh • kūl) *v.* To make fun of someone; to hold someone up as a laughingstock. *n.* The language or actions that make someone the object of mockery or cause a person to be laughed at.

    *Peter said that it is cruel to **ridicule** other people and make them laughingstocks.*

Practices

PRACTICE A

Directions: Match the meaning with the word from the word list.

WORD LIST

affinity	contemporary	convene	deference	didactic
eclectic	hypothesis	poignant	pretentious	ridicule

1. Poking fun at _____

2. Respect _____

3. Relating to teaching _____

4. Relating to pity _____

5. A possible solution to a problem _____

6. Modern _____

7. Showy _____

8. Made up of numerous sources _____

9. Assemble _____

10. Attraction to another _____

STOP. *Check answers at the back of the book on page 247.*

PRACTICE B

Directions: Define the words below.

1. Affinity _____

2. Deference _____

3. Hypothesis _____

4. Poignant _____

5. Ridicule _____

6. Convene _____

7. Contemporary _____

8. Pretentious _____

9. Eclectic _____

10. Didactic _____

STOP. *Check answers at the back of the book on page 247.*

PRACTICE C

Directions: Choose the word from the word list that *best* fits in the blank. A word may be used once only. If necessary, you may change the form of the word in the word list.

WORD LIST

affinity	contemporary	convene	deference	didactic
eclectic	hypothesis	poignant	pretentious	ridicule

1. At college, I have met a lot of people and developed a great _____ for many of them.

2. Not all the people I have met are _____ of mine.

3. I will say, however, that not one of the people I consider a friend is

   _____.

4. My friends are a(n) _____ group of people and come from different races, religions, and ethnic groups.

5. We decided that after we graduate from college, we will _____ at one of our homes.

6. In _____ to Mark, who is the oldest of our group, we agreed to meet at his house first.

7. It was quite _____ to speak of graduation, and many of my friends became misty-eyed at the thought.

8. My friends are sensitive to the feelings of others, and no one _____ or pokes fun at anyone.

9. It sounds _____ but so be it; I believe in the Golden Rule, which says that if you want others to be nice to you, you must be nice to them.

10. My friends and I would love to test the _____ that deals with random acts of kindness.

Multiple-Choice Assessment of Lessons 25–27

Directions: Words are arranged by lesson. Underline the meaning that best fits the word. Answers are presented at the back of the book. **If you miss any word meaning, go back to the lesson and restudy the word.**

LESSON 25

1. abstract
   a. concrete
   b. to state
   c. to summarize
   d. to complete

2. austere
   a. proud
   b. severe
   c. lots of ornaments
   d. happy

3. celibacy
   a. referring to priests
   b. severe
   c. unmarried
   d. sexual involvement

4. compensate
   a. save
   b. share
   c. make up for
   d. starve

5. delve
a. to search
b. to turn
c. to inform
d. to dig dirt

6. deprecate
a. to belittle
b. to help
c. to approve
d. to dig for

7. esoteric
a. easy to understand
b. to select
c. hard to understand
d. referring to belittling

8. improvise
a. to make something
b. to do on the spur of the moment
c. to help
d. to do something helpful

9. query
a. questions asked by a reporter
b. to pry
c. a question
d. to report

10. redundant
a. necessary
b. not enough
c. required information
d. unnecessary

LESSON 26

11. dire
a. extreme
b. distress
c. unnecessary
d. to cause

12. extrinsic
a. relating to
b. external
c. connected
d. necessary

13. feasible
a. related
b. complex
c. possible
d. simple

14. intrinsic
a. belonging
b. essential
c. helpful
d. dependent

15. libel
a. a liar
b. to defame someone
c. label
d. to kill someone

16. morality
a. wrong behavior
b. being righteous
c. being right
d. the principles of right conduct

17. ominous
a. evil
b. referring to clouds
c. knowing right from wrong
d. referring to a warning

18. ornate
a. simple
b. showy
c. not adorned
d. adorable

19. placid
   a. noisy
   b. calm
   c. refers to a mountain
   d. surprised

20. pragmatic
   a. practical
   b. possible
   c. probable
   d. terrible

LESSON 27

21. affinity
   a. relationship
   b. showy
   c. attractive
   d. close relationship

22. contemporary
   a. referring to furniture
   b. modern
   c. referring to peers
   d. a happening

23. convene
   a. an assembly
   b. mutually beneficial
   c. to assemble
   d. to help

24. deference
   a. an opinion
   b. a polite person
   c. a judgment
   d. respect

25. didactic
   a. related to teaching
   b. a school
   c. a teacher
   d. a student

26. eclectic
   a. mixed
   b. a mixture
   c. selecting from various sources
   d. relating to teaching

27. hypothesis
   a. the answer
   b. a possible answer
   c. a proven statement
   d. an unproved answer that
      requires further investigation

28. poignant
   a. a pitiful person
   b. arousing pity
   c. to arouse some emotion
   d. to move

29. pretentious
   a. showy
   b. making claims
   c. important
   d. a friendly person

30. ridicule
   a. to help
   b. to arouse emotion
   c. to poke fun at
   d. to laugh

STOP. *Check answers at the back of the book on page 247.*

WORDS

empirical	enervate	glib	impediment	intrepid
itinerant	latent	placate	propriety	waive

1. empirical (em • pir′ uh • kal) *adj*. Based solely on observation and experimentation rather than theory; relying on practical experience rather than on scientific principles.

*The instructor said that he believed in **empirical** evidence rather than on theory or educated guesses.*

2. enervate (en′ ur • vāt) *v*. To weaken; to deprive of strength. **Enervated** *adj*. Weakened.

*After my finals, I felt completely **enervated**.*

3. glib (glib) *adj*. Done in a smooth and easy manner, often so smooth that it is not very convincing; done in an offhanded way.

*My friends and I were suspicious of Frank because of the **glib** way in which he presented his side of the story.*

4. impediment (im • ped′ uh • munt) *n*. Anything that hinders, such as a speech defect; obstacle.

*Most people usually don't notice Stacy's speech **impediment** unless she brings it to their attention.*

5. intrepid (in • trep′ id) *adj*. Brave; not afraid; fearless; rashly bold.

*The **intrepid** workers ran into the burning building to try to rescue the trapped people.*

6. itinerant (ī • tin′ ur • unt) *n.* A person who travels from place to place. *adj.* Journey; walk.

*My friend said that when he first came to this country, he worked as an **itinerant** worker who had to go from job to job.*

7. latent (lāt′ unt) *adj.* Lying hidden within a person or thing; something that exists but is not revealed; dormant.

*Kirk said that numerous instructors told him he had **latent** ability, and they were waiting for him to reveal his talents to them.*

8. placate (plā′ kāt) *v.* Pacify; stop from being angry.

*After Jim lost the school election, we needed to **placate** those campaign workers upset about his loss.*

9. propriety (prō • prī′ uh • tē) *n.* The quality of being proper.

*Some people are very concerned with **propriety**; they like to do everything in a proper way.*

10. waive (wāv) *v.* To give up a right or claim; to relinquish something.

*At the court hearing, the defendant said that he was going to **waive** his right to an attorney.*

Practices

PRACTICE A

Directions: Match the meaning with the word from the word list.

WORD LIST

empirical	enervate	glib	impediment	intrepid
itinerant	latent	placate	propriety	waive

1. Done in a smooth and easy manner _____

2. Obstacle _____

3. Brave _____

4. Something existing but lying hidden _____

5. To give up something _____

6. Something proper _____

7. Someone who travels from place to place _____

8. To weaken _____

9. Based on experimentation and observation rather than theory _____

10. To stop from being angry _____

STOP. *Check answers at the back of the book on page 247.*

PRACTICE B

Directions: Define the words below.

1. Empirical _____

2. Enervate _____

3. Glib _____

4. Impediment _____

5. Intrepid _____

6. Itinerant _____

7. Latent _____

8. Placate _____

9. Propriety _____

10. Waive _____

STOP. *Check answers at the back of the book on page 247.*

PRACTICE C

Directions: Choose the word from the word list that *best* fits in the blank. A word may be used once only. If necessary, you may change the form of the word in the word list.

WORD LIST

empirical	enervate	glib	impediment	intrepid
itinerant	latent	placate	propriety	waive

I could not believe that the man with a speech (1)_____ was the one who helped us. He couldn't speak in a (2)_____ manner like some people I know, but he was quite a(n) (3)_____ fellow. He was a(n) (4)_____who had no known address. Even though he was quite tired and probably (5)_____, he stopped to help us when we needed it. The man wore torn and tattered clothes, but to us, he looked like an angel. We told him there was a reward for what he did, but he (6)_____ the reward. He said that (7)_____ didn't allow him to accept a reward for helping other human beings. We didn't want to make him angry, so we (8)_____ him by not pursuing the issue. It's interesting to note that if we were to look upon him in a(n) (9)_____ way, we would not really know what his (10)_____ ability was.

WORDS

accountability	assessment	authentic	deduction	equivalent
exclusive	fiscal	inclusive	intense	measurement

1. **accountability** (uh • kount′ uh • bil • uh • tē) *n.* Responsibility; the act of giving reasons for one's acts.
   *The field of education has embraced **accountability** where students and teachers must be responsible for their acts.*

2. **assessment** (uh • ses′ ment) *n.* The evaluation or diagnosis (in education); an imposing of an amount one must pay for property (real estate); an estimation of the importance or value of something.
   *The word **assessment** has several meanings when used in education.*

3. **authentic** (o • then′ tik) *adj.* Trustworthy; reliable; true; not false; genuine.
   *It seems to me that when people talk about **authentic** tests, they are talking about any test that is reliable.*

4. **deduction** (de • duk′ shun) *n.* The act of drawing a conclusion by reasoning or reasoning that goes from the general to the specific or particular; the taking away or subtraction of something; an inference or conclusion.
   *One example of **deduction** would be to give people a generalization and have them come up with examples.*

5. **equivalent** (ē • kwiv′ uh • lunt) *adj.* Equal; same.
   *When Jennifer and I shared an apartment, we paid **equivalent** amounts for our share of the rent.*

6. **exclusive** (eks • klu′ siv) *adj.* Tending to keep out all others; shutting out other considerations, happenings, and so forth; being the only one of its kind.
   *You can imagine how upset Megan and Mary were when they showed up at the party wearing the same dress, because each thought it was an **exclusive** design.*

7. fiscal (fis′ kul) *adj.* Financial; having to do with the public treasury; having to do with government policies to maintain economic stability.
*The **fiscal** policies of all states is such that they must maintain a balanced budget.*

8. inclusive (in • klū′ siv) *adj.* Taking everything and all into account.
*We are presently living in an **inclusive** society, where no one is supposed to be left out.*

9. intense (in • tens′) *adj.* Having great or extreme force; very strong; existing or occurring to a high or extreme degree.
*The heat from the fire was so **intense** that the firefighters had great difficulty entering the building.*

10. measurement (mezh′ ur • ment) *n.* The extent or capacity of something.
*In evaluation, the more **measurement** of something you have, the better the evaluation.*

Practices

PRACTICE A

Directions: Match the meaning with the word from the word list.

WORD LIST

accountability	assessment	authentic	deduction	equivalent
exclusive	fiscal	inclusive	intense	measurement

1. Financial _____

2. Real _____

3. Applies to all _____

4. Equal _____

5. Having great force _____

6. The capacity of something _____

7. An inference _____

8. Tending to keep out something _____

9. To evaluate _____

10. The act of giving reasons for one's acts _____

STOP. *Check answers at the back of the book on page 247.*

PRACTICE B

Directions: Define the words below.

1. Accountability _____

2. Authentic _____

3. Deduction _____

4. Equivalent _____

5. Assess _____

6. Inclusive _____

7. Exclusive _____

8. Fiscal _____

9. Measurement _____

10. Intense _____

STOP. *Check answers at the back of the book on page 247.*

PRACTICE C

Directions: Choose the word from the word list that *best* fits in the blank. A word may be used once only. If necessary, you may change the form of the word in the word list.

WORD LIST

accountability	assessment	authentic	deduction	equivalent
exclusive	fiscal	inclusive	intense	measurement

The word (1)_____ is very big in the twenty-first century, especially in education. Educators want to know whether students have achieved according to certain standards. Other words that are used a lot are (2)_____, which deals with estimation; (3)_____, which refers to "not fake"; and (4)_____, which means "equal." Actually, I like the word (5)_____ because it has so many meanings. I especially like when it refers to an inference or conclusion in reasoning, but my friend likes the word because it is an important part of the scientific method. It isn't (6)_____, that is, it doesn't just refer to mathematics. Actually, the word is a(n) (7)_____ one because it seems to take so many areas into account. I've been taught that evaluation is based on having lots of good (8)_____. In these (9)_____ times, when people are under lots of stress, it's important that we have a good (10)_____ policy, so we can afford to pay for all the extra expenditures.

LESSON 30

WORDS

| anthropology | astrology | astronomy | biology | civics |
| ecology | geology | philosophy | psychology | theology |

1. **anthropology** (an • thruh • pol′ uh • jē) *n.* The study of humankind; the study of the cultures and customs of people.
*In **anthropology**, we studied about a tribe of people who had an entirely different culture from ours.*

2. **astrology** (uh • strol′ uh • gē) *n.* The reading of the stars; the art or practice that claims to tell the future and interpret the influence of the heavenly bodies on the fate of people.
*Many people seem to believe in **astrology** and its ability to influence their lives.*

3. **astronomy** (uh • stron′ uh • mē) *n.* The science that deals with stars, planets, and space.
*In my **astronomy** class, I used a very high-powered telescope to view the stars.*

4. **biology** (bī • ol′ uh • jē) *n.* The science of life.
***Biology** helps people learn about living things.*

5. **civics** (siv′ iks) *n.* (Used in the singular) The part of political science that deals with the study of the rights and responsibilities of citizenship; the part of political science that deal with citizens' affairs.
*Because I am very concerned about citizens' rights, I thought that it would be a good idea to take a course in **civics**.*

6. **ecology** (ē kol′ uh • jē) *n.* The study of the relationship between living organisms and their environment.
*Ed said that he was interested in the environment, so he is taking courses in **ecology**.*

7. **geology** (jē • ol′ uh • jē) *n*. Study of the earth's physical history and makeup.
*My friend Mike is studying **geology** because he is interested in rocks and their formations.*

8. **philosophy** (fi • los′ uh • fē) *n*. The study of human knowledge; the love of wisdom and the search for it; a search for the general laws that give a reasonable explanation of something.
*Students of **philosophy** are interested in understanding various ideas better.*

9. **psychology** (sī kol′ uh • jē) *n*. The science dealing with mental processes and the mind; the science dealing with human and animal behavior.
*Teachers usually take **psychology** courses to learn more about human behavior.*

10. **theology** (thē • ol′ uh • jē) *n*. The study of religion.
*Those who wish to learn more about religion must take courses in **theology**.*

Practices

PRACTICE A

Directions: Match the meaning with the word from the word list.

WORD LIST

anthropology	astrology	astronomy	biology	civics
ecology	geology	philosophy	psychology	theology

1. The study of the mind _____

2. The study of religion _____

3. The study of life _____

4. That part of political science dealing with citizens' affairs _____

5. The study of human knowledge _____

6. The study of the relationship between the environment and living organisms

_____

7. The study of the earth's physical history and makeup _____

8. The study dealing with the stars _____

9. The reading of the stars _____

10. The study of humankind _____

> **STOP.** *Check answers at the back of the book on page 247.*

PRACTICE B

Directions: Define the words below.

1. Anthropology _____

2. Astrology _____

3. Astronomy _____

4. Biology _____

5. Civics _____

6. Ecology _____

7. Geology _____

8. Philosophy _____

9. Psychology _____

10. Theology _____

> **STOP.** *Check answers at the back of the book on pages 247–248.*

PRACTICE C

Directions: Choose the word from the word list that *best* fits in the blank. A word may be used once only. If necessary, you may also change the form of the word in the word list.

WORD LIST

| anthropology | astrology | astronomy | biology | civics |
| ecology | geology | philosophy | psychology | theology |

At college, there are so many courses that I don't know what I want to major in. I

thought at first that I would major in (1) _____ because I was very interested in living things. However, when my father bought me a telescope, I became interested in (2)_____. Would you believe that my school actually has a course in (3)_____, which is a false science? It seems that many people are interested in reading their horoscopes. I kept changing what I want to major in. When I took a course in religion, I thought that I would major in (4)_____. During the elections, I decided to major in (5)_____. There was a time when (6)_____ appealed to me because I was interested in human behavior. Of course, (7)_____ also appealed to me because I love to learn about human knowledge. When we discussed the environment, I was sure that I wanted to major in (8)_____. And when we discussed (9)_____, which is the study of humankind, I wanted to spend my life researching various tribes and their cultures. Would you believe that I still do not know what I want to major in? Perhaps I'll major in (10)_____ because last year I was involved in mountain climbing. I really don't know what I want to do with the rest of my life. Right now, I'm just taking lots of courses in many different areas.

Multiple-Choice Assessment of Lessons 28–30

Directions: Words are arranged by lesson. Underline the meaning that *best* fits the word. Answers are at the end of the book. **If you miss any word meaning, go back to the lesson and restudy the word.**

LESSON 28

1. empirical
   a. confused
   b. based on experimentation
   c. educated guesses
   d. purely theoretical

2. enervate
   a. to weaken
   b. to give energy to
   c. to strengthen
   d. to experiment

3. glib
   a. done roughly
   b. done correctly
   c. done in an offhand way
   d. powerful

4. impediment
   a. refers to speech
   b. anything that hinders
   c. refers to injuries
   d. encouragement

5. intrepid
   a. afraid
   b. rash
   c. not afraid
   d. fearful

6. itinerant
   a. a worker
   b. a traveler
   c. to wander
   d. going on foot

7. latent
   a. refers to paint
   b. something not showy
   c. sleeping
   d. dormant

8. placate
   a. something that helps
   b. to place
   c. to calm
   d. to make angry

9. propriety
   a. refers to quality
   b. refers to being proper
   c. refers to health
   d. refers to someone's beliefs

10. waive
   a. to wave
   b. to right a wrong
   c. to give up something
   d. to claim something

LESSON 29

11. accountability
   a. a reason
   b. one's acts
   c. a test
   d. responsibility

12. assessment
   a. tests
   b. refers to real estate
   c. refers to education
   d. to evaluate

13. authentic
   a. real
   b. untrue
   c. refers to tests
   d. false

14. deduction
   a. going from specific to general
   b. refers to electricity
   c. a general
   d. reasoning ability

15. equivalent
   a. different
   b. same
   c. refers to math
   d. false

16. exclusive
   a. happenings
   b. closing
   c. tending to keep all others out
   d. similar

17. fiscal
   a. financial
   b. strong
   c. the government's policies
   d. feelings

18. inclusive
   a. all
   b. taking all into account
   c. account
   d. keeping others out

19. intense
   a. having heat
   b. tense
   c. having extreme force
   d. refers to headache

20. measurement
   a. capacity of something
   b. refers to finance
   c. account
   d. refers to all

LESSON 30

21. anthropology
   a. refers to ants
   b. refers to a science
   c. the study of ants
   d. the study of humankind

22. astrology
   a. refers to a science
   b. refers to humans
   c. the reading of the stars
   d. refers to science travel

23. astronomy
   a. the study of the stars
   b. space travel
   c. stars
   d. the science of life

24. biology
   a. a science
   b. refers to life
   c. living things
   d. the science of life

25. civics
   a. part of political science
   b. the study of citizens
   c. deals with citizens
   d. study that deals with
      citizens' affairs

26. ecology
   a. relationships
   b. living organisms
   c. the study of relationships
   d. study of relations between
      environment and living
      organisms

27. geology
   a. refers to rocks and their
      formation
   b. concerned with living things
   c. the study of the earth's physical
      history
   d. a physical history

28. philosophy
   a. refers to wisdom
   b. the study of knowledge
   c. the study of the mind
   d. the study of mental faculties

29. psychology
   a. the science of wisdom
   b. love of knowledge
   c. the science of the mind
   d. mental disorders

30. theology
   a. refers to religion
   b. the study of religion
   c. religious clerics
   d. refers to priests and other
      religious persons

STOP. *Check answers at the back of the book on page 248.*

WORDS

ambiguous	belligerent	civil	civilian	civilization
novice	pacify	politics	posthumously	provoke

1. **ambiguous** (am • big′ ū • us) *adj.* Having two or more meanings.
   *Some people use **ambiguous** language on purpose; they don't want others to know exactly what they are saying.*

2. **belligerent** (buh • lij′ uh • runt) *adj.* Warlike. *n.* Any nation, group, or person engaged in fighting or war.
   *At school, we avoid any person who behaves in a **belligerent** manner.*

3. **civil** (siv′ul) *adj.* Polite or courteous; pertaining to citizens and their government; relating to ordinary community life as distinguished from military or church affairs.
   *I feel that it is important to behave in a **civil** manner, even when we disagree with others.*

4. **civilian** (si • vil′ yun) *n.* Someone not in the military. *adj.* Relating to those not in the military.
   *My friend said that after spending three years in the military, he was looking forward to being a **civilian** again.*

5. **civilization** (siv′ uh • luh • zā • shun) *n.* A state of human society that has a high level of intellectual, social, and cultural development; the cultural development of a specific people, country, or region.
   *A **civilization** is supposed to have a high level of intellectual, social, and cultural development.*

6. novice (nov' is) *n.* A beginner; someone new at something; a rookie.
*Even though Kim is a **novice** at tennis, you would never know it from watching her play.*

7. pacify (pas' uh • fī) *v.* To bring peace to; to calm; to quiet.
*My friend Karl tried to **pacify** the crowd, but he couldn't calm the people down.*

8. politics (pol' uh • tiks) *n.* (Although plural, it is usually looked upon as singular.) The science and art of government or the management and direction of public and state affairs.
Politics has gotten such a bad name that some able people don't go into the management of public or state affairs.

9. posthumously (pos' chū • mus • lē) *adv.* After death.
*It's unfortunate that numerous artists gain recognition for their works **posthumously**, that is, after their death.*

10. provoke (pruh • vōk') *v.* To irritate; to stir up anger or resentment.
*The speaker so **provoked** some people in the audience that they stood up and booed.*

Practices

PRACTICE A

Directions: Match the meaning with the word from the word list.

WORD LIST

ambiguous	belligerent	civil	civilian	civilization
novice	pacify	politics	posthumously	provoke

1. Confusing _____

2. After death _____

3. A rookie _____

4. To irritate _____

5. Warlike _____

6. Polite _____

7. To calm _____

8. One not in the military _____

9. Cultural development of a people _____

10. The science of government _____

STOP. *Check answers at the back of the book on page 248.*

PRACTICE B

Directions: Choose a word from this lesson that *best* fits the meaning of the italicized word or words in each sentence.

1. It's sad that some people become well-known only *after death*.

2. We were frightened when the *warlike* men approached us in a menacing way. _____

3. My parents taught me to be *polite* to people. _____

4. After I left the army, it felt good to be a *person out of the military*. _____

5. I try not to *irritate* people, but at times I seem to do so. _____

6. It upsets me when my instructor gives us *confusing* directions about an assignment. _____

7. My friends said that because I was a *beginner* at the game, they would overlook some of my errors. _____

8. My sister, Claudia, said that she wanted to go into government service where she would deal with *the art of government*. _____

9. At the school rally, some people got so rowdy that we had to *calm them down*. _____

10. We studied *the cultural development of many nations* in our anthropology class. _____

STOP. *Check answers at the back of the book on page 248.*

PRACTICE C

Directions: Match the number of the word in Column A with the letter of its meaning in Column B.

	Column A	*Column B*
_____	1. ambiguous	a. to calm
_____	2. belligerent	b. someone not in the military
_____	3. civil	c. a beginner
_____	4. civilian	d. having two or more meanings
_____	5. civilization	e. after death
_____	6. novice	f. the science and art of government
_____	7. pacify	g. warlike
_____	8. politics	h. to irritate
_____	9. posthumously	i. polite
_____	10. provoke	j. cultural development of a country

LESSON 32

WORDS

defer	diffident	dissent	divulge	dormant
hypertension	lucid	morbidity	mortality	procrastinate

1. defer (dē • fer′) *v.* To put off or delay; to put off for a future time; to yield in opinion to someone out of respect for the person.
*We often **defer** to the dean of our school when he speaks.*

2. diffident (dif′ uh • dunt) *adj.* Shy; timid; lacking confidence.
*From observing how outgoing Kate is today, you would never believe that as a child she was so **diffident**.*

3. dissent (di • sent′) *v.* To differ in belief or opinion to someone else; to disagree.
*Even though we **dissented** from his opinions, we let him speak.*

4. divulge (duh • vulj′) *v.* To disclose; reveal; to make known.
*My mother always told me that if I didn't want everyone to know my secrets, I should not **divulge** them to even one person.*

5. dormant (dor′ munt) *adj.* Sleeping; inactive; quiet; still.
*The volcano had been **dormant** for so long that no one could ever remember it erupting.*

6. hypertension (hī • pur • ten′ shun) *n.* High blood pressure.
***Hypertension** is often referred to as a silent killer because many people do not know that they have high blood pressure.*

7. lucid (lū′ sid) *adj.* Clear; easily understood; shining; bright.
*Some instructors do not know how to give a **lucid** answer when asked to explain something.*

146

8. morbidity (mor • bid′ uh • tē) *n.* Rate of disease or proportion of diseased people in a certain locality.

*The **morbidity** of some people whose parents have died of a certain disease is high.*

9. mortality (mor • tal′ uh • tē) *n.* Death rate; the state of someone having to eventually die; proportion of people dying in a certain locality.

*It makes sense that the **mortality** of children in all socioeconomic groups depends on the care they receive.*

10. procrastinate (prō • kras′ tuh • nāt) *v.* To postpone taking action; to put off doing something until a future time.

*If you **procrastinate** doing the research for your paper, you will never get it written on time.*

SHOE reprinted by permission of Tribune Media Services.

Practices

PRACTICE A

Directions: Match the meaning with the words from the word list.

WORD LIST

defer	diffident	dissent	divulge	dormant
hypertension	lucid	morbidity	mortality	procrastinate

1. To yield in opinion to another _____

2. To postpone taking action until a future time _____

3. To disagree _____

4. Sleeping _____

5. Shy _____

6. Reveal _____

7. Disease rate _____

8. Death rate _____

9. High blood pressure _____

10. Clear _____

> **STOP.** *Check answers at the back of the book on page 248.*

PRACTICE B

Directions: Choose a word from this lesson that *best* fits the meaning of the *italicized* word or words in each sentence.

1. What you are saying is not very *clear.* _____

2. Must you *reveal* that information to everyone? _____

3. The bear is usually *inactive* in the winter. _____

4. Jim always *puts off for a later time* any school work he has to do. _____

5. According to the actuary tables, the *death rate* of men hasn't really changed much in the past few decades. _____

6. Do males or females have a higher *disease rate?* _____

7. *High blood pressure* can be very dangerous if it goes unchecked. _____

8. When Maria was a young child, she was very *shy.* _____

9. My roommate always seems ready to *disagree* with whatever I say. _____

10. I always seem to *yield in opinion to someone out of respect for the person* even if I do not agree with what he or she is saying. _____

> **STOP.** *Check answers at the back of the book on page 248.*

PRACTICE C

Directions: Match the number of the word in Column A to the letter of its meaning in Column B.

	Column A	*Column B*
_____	1. defer	a. to make known
_____	2. diffident	b. inactive
_____	3. dissent	c. shy
_____	4. divulge	d. to put off
_____	5. dormant	e. death rate
_____	6. hypertension	f. rate of disease
_____	7. lucid	g. to postpone
_____	8. morbidity	h. clear
_____	9. mortality	i. high blood pressure
_____	10. procrastinate	j. to disagree

33

WORDS

agnostic	archaic	atheist	bigamy	egocentric
generic	indictment	innovation	misanthrope	monogamy

1. **agnostic** (ag • nos′ tik) *n.* A person who is not for or against something; one who claims uncertainty; one who doubts that the ultimate cause (God) and the essential nature of things are knowable.
   *An **agnostic** is not sure of certain things.*

2. **archaic** (ar • kā′ ik) *adj.* Ancient; belonging to an earlier period; old-fashioned; no longer used.
   *Bloodletting for curing disease is an **archaic** method that is no longer used.*

3. **atheist** (ā′ thē • ist) *n.* One who doesn't believe in the existence of God.
   *An **atheist** does not believe in the existence of God.*

4. **bigamy** (big′ uh • mē) *n.* Marriage to two spouses at the same time.
   ***Bigamy** is outlawed in the United States, so the person who was married to two spouses at the same time is now in prison.*

5. **egocentric** (ē • gō • sen′ trik) *adj.* Self-centered; relating everything to oneself.
   *Megan said that she dislikes people who are so **egocentric** that they begin practically every sentence with "I."*

6. **generic** (juh • ner′ ik) *adj.* Referring to all in a group or class.
   *When people today say "all men," they are usually speaking in a **generic** sense, that is, they are referring to both men and women.*

7. indictment (in • dīt′ munt) *n.* A charge; an accusation.

*An **indictment** is an accusation that a person committed a crime, but in our country, a person is considered innocent until proven guilty.*

8. innovation (in • uh • vā′ shun) *n.* Something newly introduced; something new; a new method.

*Have you noticed that once a drug can be sold without a doctor's prescription, drug companies develop **innovations** to it so that it again requires a doctor's prescription?*

9. misanthrope (mis′ an • thrōp) *n.* Hater of humankind.

*A **misanthrope** is a hater of all people, so Bill cannot be one, because he likes women.*

10. monogamy (muh • nog′ uh • mē) *n.* Marriage to one spouse at one time.

*In the United States, we believe in **monogamy**, whereby you are married to one spouse at one time.*

Practices

PRACTICE A

Directions: Define the words below.

1. Agnostic _____

2. Archaic _____

3. Atheist _____

4. Bigamy _____

5. Egocentric _____

6. Generic _____

7. Indictment _____

8. Innovation _____

9. Misanthrope _____

10. Monogamy _____

STOP. *Check answers at the back of the book on page 248.*

PRACTICE B

Directions: Match the meaning with the word from the word list.

WORD LIST

agnostic	archaic	atheist	bigamy	egocentric
generic	indictment	innovation	misanthrope	monogamy

1. Married to two spouses at the same time _____

2. Concerned primarily with oneself _____

3. Married to one spouse at a time _____

4. Does not believe in God _____

5. Is unsure about the existence of God _____

6. Something new _____

7. Refers to something old _____

8. Hater of humankind _____

9. Refers to all _____

10. A charge or accusation _____

> **STOP.** *Check answers at the back of the book on page 248.*

PRACTICE C

Directions: Choose the word from the word list that *best* fits in the blank. A word may be used once only. If necessary, you may change the form of the word in the word list.

WORD LIST

agnostic	archaic	atheist	bigamy	egocentric
generic	indictment	innovation	misanthrope	monogamy

Melinda believes in (1)_____, that is, marriage to one person at a time. You can imagine how upset she was to learn that her spouse was involved in (2)_____. When Melinda married Jason, he claimed that he was a(n) (3)_____. Melinda said that she would respect Jason's right not to believe in any god. She also claimed to be a(n) (4)_____, that is, she didn't know whether there was or wasn't a god.

Recently, however, Jason kept going out at night, and when Melinda asked him where he was going, Jason would say that he was going to church. Melinda thought that after ten years of marriage, she knew Jason pretty well. She knew that he was a(n) (5)_____, a person who didn't like people, as well as a(n) (6)_____ person who only thought of himself. She also knew that Jason often spoke of himself in a(n) (7)_____ or general sense and that he enjoyed new things, that is, (8)_____. It's because of the latter and how Jason had been behaving toward her lately that she decided to follow him. She knew that her behavior seemed (9)_____, that is, not very modern but actually old-fashioned. However, she had been brought up in a traditional family where divorce was usually frowned on. Also, it would be difficult to make a(n) (10)_____ against her husband unless she had proof and knew what he was doing.

Multiple-Choice Assessment of Lessons 31–33

Directions: Words are arranged by lesson. Underline the meaning that *best* fits the word. Answers are at the back of the book. **If you miss any word meaning, go back to the lesson and restudy the word.**

LESSON 31

1. ambiguous
   a. confusing
   b. confusing on purpose
   c. meanings
   d. having no meaning

2. belligerent
   a. friendly
   b. pretty
   c. an enemy
   d. warlike

3. civil
   a. enemies
   b. polite
   c. culture
   d. warlike

4. civilian
   a. not in uniform
   b. in the military
   c. polite person
   d. not in the military

5. civilization
   a. culture
   b. human society
   c. cultural development of a people
   d. interested in cultural endeavors

6. novice
   a. rookie
   b. a person who likes to read
   c. refers to a novel
   d. an inventor

7. **pacify**
   a. a quiet person
   b. not interested in war
   c. to calm
   d. to declare victory

8. **politics**
   a. a crook
   b. the art of governing
   c. refers to politicians
   d. the government

9. **posthumously**
   a. refers to something funny
   b. putting off things to do
   c. after death
   d. refers to the mail

10. **provoke**
    a. to stamp out
    b. to irritate
    c. to fight
    d. to destroy

LESSON 32

11. **defer**
    a. to honor
    b. to delay
    c. to harm
    d. refers to someone elderly

12. **diffident**
    a. lacking
    b. indifferent
    c. shy
    d. refers to being different

13. **dissent**
    a. refers to sun rays
    b. distance
    c. refers to distance
    d. to disagree

14. **divulge**
    a. to reveal
    b. to eat a lot
    c. to keep secret
    d. to swallow

15. **dormant**
    a. active
    b. to calm
    c. refers to bears
    d. inactive

16. **hypertension**
    a. secret weapon
    b. a silent killer
    c. high blood pressure
    d. tense

17. **lucid**
    a. easy to listen
    b. easily understood
    c. easy to speak
    d. not easy to understand

18. **morbidity**
    a. rate of disease
    b. depressed
    c. a disease
    d. sad

19. **mortality**
    a. disease rate
    b. heart rate
    c. death rate
    d. refers to death

20. **procrastinate**
    a. to hurry
    b. to postpone taking action until
       a later date
    c. to decide
    d. to take action immediately

LESSON 33

21. agnostic
  a. a person who believes
  b. a confused person
  c. one who claims uncertainty
  d. a person who refuses help

22. archaic
  a. refers to an old person
  b. old books
  c. ancient
  d. old fashioned views

23. atheist
  a. a nonbeliever
  b. a religious person
  c. a nonbeliever in God's existence
  d. an uncertain person

24. bigamy
  a. married
  b. married to two spouses at the same time
  c. refers to marriage vows
  d. married to two spouses at different times

25. egocentric
  a. the earth as the center
  b. refers to the center
  c. the self as the center
  d. the center of all things

26. generic
  a. referring to all
  b. something
  c. something everyone wants
  d. a class

27. indictment
  a. to find someone guilty
  b. a trial
  c. to fine a person
  d. a charge

28. innovation
  a. refers to a novel
  b. an introduction
  c. something new
  d. a new drug

29. misanthrope
  a. a hater
  b. a hater of humankind
  c. a hater of women
  d. a dog hater

30. monogamy
  a. refers to marriage
  b. marriage to one spouse at one time
  c. marriage to a few people
  d. marriage to more than one spouse at the same time

STOP. *Check answers at the back of the book on page 248.*

LESSON 34

WORDS

anachronism	avocation	demography	innate	magnanimous
megalopolis	recession	tenacious	vocal	vocation

1. anachronism (uh • nak′ ruh • niz • um) *n.* Something out of time order; an error in chronology (the science of measuring time in fixed periods and arranging dates in their proper order) in which a person, an object, or an event is assigned an incorrect date or period.
*An example of an **anachronism** would be to have someone wearing a watch in a film about the Stone Age.*

2. avocation (av • uh • kā′ shun) *n.* A hobby; something people do in addition to their regular work, usually for enjoyment.
*Peter claims that playing tennis is his **avocation**.*

3. demography (de • mog′ ruh • fē) *n.* The statistical study of human populations, including births, deaths, marriages, population movements, and so on.
*The census bureau tries to determine the **demography** of our country every ten years.*

4. innate (i • nāt′) *adj.* Born with; inborn; not acquired from the environment; beginning in; coming from; belonging to the fundamental nature of something.
*An **innate** characteristic is something you have had since birth.*

5. magnanimous (mag • nan′ uh • mus) *adj.* Forgiving of insults or injuries; highminded; great of spirit.
*A **magnanimous** person usually will overlook insults that are hurled at him or her.*

6. **megalopolis** (meg • uh • lop′ uh • lus) *n.* One very large city made up of a number of cities; a vast, populous, continuously urban area.

The area between Boston and Washington, D.C., is considered a ***megalopolis*** *because of the high density of population between these two cities.*

7. **recession** (ri • sesh′ un) *n.* The act of going back; in economics, the decline of business activity.

In a ***recession*** *when unemployment is high, economists try to think of ways to stimulate the economy.*

8. **tenacious** (tuh • nā′ shus) *adj.* Tough; holding or strongly holding to one's views; opinions, rights, and so forth; stubborn; retentive.

When Jack makes up his mind about something, he is so ***tenacious*** *about his feelings that it is almost impossible to try and change his mind.*

9. **vocal** (vō′ kul) *adj.* Oral; freely expressing oneself in speech, usually with force; speaking out; referring to the voice.

Be careful not to be too ***vocal*** *at the ballgame because you could lose your voice.*

10. **vocation** (vō • kā′ shun) *n.* A calling; a person's work or profession.

Maria chose medicine as her ***vocation***.

Practices

PRACTICE A

Directions: Define the words below.

1. Anachronism _____

2. Avocation _____

3. Demography _____

4. Innate _____

5. Magnanimous _____

6. Megalopolis _____

7. Recession _____

8. Tenacious _____

9. Vocal _____

10. Vocation _____

> **STOP.** *Check answers at the back of the book on page 248.*

PRACTICE B

Directions: Match the meaning with the word from the word list.

WORD LIST

anachronism	avocation	demography	innate	magnanimous
megalopolis	recession	tenacious	vocal	vocation

1. A person's job _____

2. A person's hobby _____

3. Great of spirit _____

4. Stubborn _____

5. Using one's voice strongly _____

6. Inborn _____

7. Refers to population _____

8. One great city _____

9. Something out of time order _____

10. A slowing down of economic activity _____

> **STOP.** *Check answers at the back of the book on page 248.*

PRACTICE C

Directions: Choose the word from the word list that *best* fits in the blank. A word may be used once only. If necessary, you may change the form of the word in the word list.

WORD LIST

anachronism	avocation	demography	innate	magnanimous
megalopolis	recession	tenacious	vocal	vocation

1. Even though this is not the _____ I planned to pursue, it is the only work I could get.

2. The singer said that she was unhappy with the orchestra because it was too loud, and she felt that if she sang any louder, it would hurt her _____ cords.

3. I do not have any special _____, but I do like to read.

4. The area between large cities is often considered one _____.

5. It is a(n) _____ to have people wearing watches in a film set in the Middle Ages.

6. The _____ of a population is used often to determine the trends of vital statistics.

7. Almost everyone knows that _____ characteristics are those with which you are born.

8. I thought that he was very _____ to overlook all the insults that were thrown at him during his speech.

9. It really seems silly for Joshua to have such _____ feelings on something that he can't do anything about.

10. During a(n) _____ there is usually high unemployment.

WORDS

agile	approbation	centennial	centimeter	decameter
decimate	decimeter	kilometer	megabit	millennium

1. **agile** (aj′ īl) *adj.* Quick and easy of movement; keen and lively.
   *Meg has a very **agile** wit; she is so quick to come up with the right words at the right moment.*

2. **approbation** (ap • ruh • bā′ shun) *n.* Official approval, support, or commendation.
   *At college, many of my friends seem to need the **approbation** of their instructors.*

3. **centennial** (sen • ten′ ē • ul) *adj.* Referring to a period of 100 years; lasting years; *n.* A one-hundredth anniversary.
   *In our history course, we learned that the **centennial** celebration of our nation took place in 1876.*

4. **centimeter** (sent′ uh • mēt • ur) *n.* In the metric system, a unit of measure equal to $\frac{1}{100}$ meter (0.3937 inch).
   *Our instructor had us measure the distance in **centimeters** because he wanted us to know it to the nearest hundredth of a meter.*

5. **decameter** (dek′ uh • mēt • ur) *n.* A decameter equals ten meters.
   *When you travel abroad, you should know that a **decameter** is equal to ten meters.*

6. **decimate** (des′ uh • māt) *v.* To take or destroy a tenth part of; to destroy but not completely; to destroy a great number or proportion of.
   *If you are in an earthquake or flood, it is better for your home to be **decimated** than obliterated because you do not completely lose everything.*

7. **decimeter** (des′ uh • mēt • ur) *n.* In the metric system, a unit of length equal to ¹/₁₀ meter.
*Because a **decimeter** is about 4 inches, it would take approximately 3 **decimeters** to equal 1 foot.*

8. **kilometer** (kil′ uh • mēt • ur) *n.* A **kilometer** equals 1000 meters.
*Because a **kilometer** is equal to 1000 meters, it is about 0.62 of a mile.*

9. **megabit** (meg′ uh • bit) A megabit equals 1,000,000 bits.
*Because a bit is a unit of computer information, and 1 byte equals 8 bits of data, and a word usually equals 2 bytes, or 16 bits, of data, it's important to have at least a certain number of **megabits** in your computer.*

10. **millennium** (mi • len′ ē • um) *n.* Period of 1000 years; a one-thousandth anniversary; a period of great happiness.
*Another **millennium** passed when we entered the twenty-first century.*

Practices

PRACTICE A

Directions: Define the following words.

1. Agile _____

2. Approbation _____

3. Centennial _____

4. Centimeter _____

5. Decameter _____

6. Decimate _____

7. Decimeter _____

8. Kilometer _____

9. Megabit _____

10. Millennium _____

STOP. *Check answers at the back of the book on pages 248–249.*

PRACTICE B

Directions: Match the meaning with the word from the word list.

WORD LIST

agile	approbation	centennial	centimeter	decameter
decimate	decimeter	kilometer	megabit	millennium

1. 1,000,000 bits _____

2. A period of great happiness _____

3. 100 year anniversary _____

4. Official approval _____

5. Easy of movement _____

6. Equals 1000 meters _____

7. To destroy but not completely _____

8. 10 meters _____

9. One-tenth meter _____

10. $1/100$ meter _____

> **STOP.** *Check answers at the back of the book on page 249.*

PRACTICE C

Directions: Choose the word from the word list that *best* fits in the blank. A word may be used once only. If necessary, you may change the form of the word in the word list.

WORD LIST

agile	approbation	centennial	centimeter	decameter
decimate	decimeter	kilometer	megabit	millennium

1. Bethany has such a(n) _____ mind that she can answer most problems rather quickly.

2. In 1876, we in the United States celebrated our _____ birthday.

3. Some people get confused with the metric system word _____ that means 10 meters.

4. Lately, I have noticed that many people are using the word _____,
which has as one of its meanings "not to destroy completely."

5. Many students avoid peer disapproval; it appears that most want the
_____ of their peers.

6. A(n) _____ in the metric system is a unit of length equal
to 1000 meters.

7. When you need to know something to the nearest hundredth of a meter, it makes
sense to measure it in _____.

8. Memory storage is imperative in a computer, so I'm happy I have so many
_____ in my computer.

9. Pat said that she was happy to be alive in the _____, a time
known for its great happiness.

10. A(n) _____ is in the metric system and equal to $1/10$ meter.

WORDS

ambidextrous	détente	detention	equivocate	expound
harangue	irrevocable	posterity	supine	vociferous

1. ambidextrous (am • bē • dek′ strus) *adj.* Able to use both hands equally well.

*When Mike plays ball, he plays primarily with his right hand, but he writes with his left one because he is **ambidextrous**.*

2. détente (dā • tant′) *n.* The easing of strained relations, especially between nations.

*The president said that **détente** would exist between the two nations if they lived up to their agreements.*

3. detention (di • ten′ shun) *n.* Confinement; the state of being held in jail; a keeping or holding back.

*Students who receive **detention** usually have to stay after school.*

4. equivocate (i • kwiv′ uh • kāt) *v.* To use ambiguous language on purpose.

*Have you noticed how Bill always **equivocates** when he doesn't want anyone to know how he really feels about something?*

5. expound (ik • spound′) *v.* To state in detail; to explain; to set forth.

*Please **expound** further on your views so I can understand them better.*

6. harangue (huh • rang′) *n.* A ranting and inflated speech or writing. *v.* To make a ranting and inflated speech.

*When the speaker **harangued** all of us in his pompous manner, we could not wait to leave the auditorium.*

7. irrevocable (ir • rev′ uh • kuh • bul) *adj.* Not able to be altered or changed back.

*Our instructor said that the schedule of classes had been set and was **irrevocable**.*

8. posterity (pos • ter′ uh • tē) *n.* Future generations; all of one's descendants or offspring.

*Jim said that as an artist, nobody wanted his artwork now, but it would be admired in **posterity**.*

9. supine (sū′ pīn) *adj.* Lying on the back with face upward.

*When Charles lies in a **supine** position while asleep, he usually snores.*

10. vociferous (vō • sif′ ur • us) *adj.* Of forceful, aggressive, and loud speech; marked by a loud outcry; clamorous or noisy.

*Our neighbors at the dormitory were so **vociferous** that we called campus security to complain about the noise.*

Practices

PRACTICE A

Directions: Define the following words.

1. Ambidextrous _____

2. Détente _____

3. Detention _____

4. Equivocate _____

5. Expound _____

6. Harangue _____

7. Irrevocable _____

8. Posterity _____

9. Supine _____

10. Vociferous _____

STOP. *Check answers at the back of the book on page 249.*

PRACTICE B

Directions: Match the meaning with the word from the word list.

WORD LIST

ambidextrous	détente	detention	equivocate	expound
harangue	irrevocable	posterity	supine	vociferous

1. Clamorous _____

2. A ranting speech _____

3. Confinement _____

4. To use ambiguous language on purpose _____

5. To lie on one's back _____

6. Able to use both hands equally well _____

7. Not able to be changed _____

8. Future generations _____

9. The easing of strained relations _____

10. To state in detail _____

STOP. *Check answers at the back of the book on page 249.*

PRACTICE C

Directions: **Choose the word from the word list that** *best* **fits in the blank. A word may be used once only. If necessary, you may change the form of the word in the word list.**

WORD LIST

ambidextrous	détente	detention	equivocate	expound
harangue	irrevocable	posterity	supine	vociferous

1. Kelsey said that she does not like it when people _____ her to do things that she was getting ready to do.

2. The stranger was very_____ in demanding that we pay attention to him at the board meeting.

3. My brother is always ready to _____ his views on anything and everything.

4. An artist I know said that she wants to become famous in the present rather than in _____.

5. It seems that we have good _____ between our nation and England.

6. Politicians usually _____ when they don't want the public to know how they feel on an issue.

7. I am _____, so I can use both my hands equally well.

8. We were told that we could complain as much as we wanted, but the schedule was _____ and would not be changed.

9. Her spouse is in _____ at the local jail.

10. Many novelists use the word _____ when they write that a character is lying on his or her back.

Multiple-Choice Assessment of Lessons 34–36

Directions: Words are arranged by lesson. Underline the meaning that *best* fits the word. Answers are at the end of the book. **If you miss any word meaning, go back to the lesson and restudy the word.**

LESSON 34

1. anachronism
   a. out of time order
   b. one who professes
   c. someone ancient
   d. one who is sure of things

2. avocation
   a. ancient
   b. refers to words
   c. a hobby
   d. likes to be old-fashioned

3. demography
   a. one who professes
   b. one who doesn't believe in God
   c. refers to populations
   d. study of populations

4. innate
   a. refers to birth
   b. inborn
   c. refers to birth order
   d. refers to ancient times

5. magnanimous
   a. self-centered
   b. always relating
      to others
   c. great of spirit
   d. concerned

6. megalopolis
   a. refers to a group
   b. refers to cities
   c. refers to great things
   d. one large city formed by many
      cities

7. recession
   a. someone found guilty
   b. a charge
   c. the act of going back
   d. a jury trial

8. tenacious
   a. tough
   b. a method
   c. an idea
   d. a new method

9. vocal
   a. refers to freedom
   b. a hater of women
   c. oral
   d. a hater of humankind

10. vocation
   a. a person's job
   b. refers to a person
   c. to call someone
   d. to vacation

LESSON 35

11. agile
   a. easy movement
   b. an art show
   c. refers to movement
   d. refers to age

12. approbation
   a. probing
   b. refers to goods
   c. official approval
   d. nice

13. centennial
   a. an anniversary
   b. something that lasts
   c. lasting 1000 years
   d. lasting for 100 years

14. centimeter
   a. a measurement
   b. equal to $1/100$ meter
   c. in the metric system
   d. a unit of measure

15. decameter
   a. equal to $1/100$ meter
   b. in the metric system
   c. equal to $1/10$ meter
   d. equal to 10 meters

16. decimate
   a. to destroy
   b. to destroy but not completely
   c. to annihilate
   d. to erase something

17. decimeter
   a. a measurement
   b. 10 meters
   c. in the metric system
   d. $1/10$ meter

18. kilometer
   a. in the metric system
   b. 1000 meters
   c. refers to mileage
   d. $1/1000$ meter

19. megabit
   a. equals 1,000,000 bits
   b. equals 1000 bits
   c. unit of computer information
   d. refers to computer capacity

20. millennium
   a. a period of 100 years
   b. a country's anniversary
   c. a period of 1000 years
   d. a period of many years

LESSON 36

21. ambidextrous
   a. able to use both hands
   b. able to use both hands equally well
   c. able to play ball well
   d. able to eat with both hands

22. détente
   a. tense
   b. refers to a nation's tension
   c. easing of tension
   d. strained relations

23. detention
   a. confinement
   b. in jail
   c. after school activities
   d. unable to pay attention

24. equivocate
   a. refers to speech
   b. refers to language
   c. confusing on purpose
   d. a spoken message

25. expound
    a. to have something to say
    b. to state in detail
    c. what professors do
    d. to speak

26. harangue
    a. to confuse
    b. to rant about something
    c. to confuse on purpose
    d. to speak on a subject

27. irrevocable
    a. changed
    b. to change back
    c. not able to be altered
    d. to remove

28. posterity
    a. refers to posture
    b. future generations
    c. refers to the past
    d. helping one's offspring

29. supine
    a. to irritate
    b. to lie on one's back
    c. refers to one's supper
    d. not able to be changed

30. vociferous
    a. refers to voice
    b. an aggressive person
    c. loud speech
    d. to irritate

STOP. *Check answers at the back of the book on page 249.*

LESSON 37

animate	animus	depose	dictum	disposition
diverse	dogma	furtive	heterogeneous	homogeneous

1. animate (an' uh • māt) *v.* To move to action; to make alive.
*When my instructor teaches, she becomes so **animated** that every part of her becomes alive and active.*

2. animus (an' uh • mus) *n.* A feeling of strong ill will; animosity.
*I was shocked when someone I thought was a friend told me he had great **animus** toward me because I thought he liked me.*

3. depose (di • pōz') *v.* To remove from a high position such as a throne; to let fall.
*After they **deposed** their king from the throne, they banished him from the country.*

4. dictum (dik' tum) *n.* A saying; an authoritative statement.
*Although some politicians express their **dictums** as fact, they are only opinions.*

5. disposition (dis • puh • zish' un) *n.* A natural tendency; one's usual frame of mind or one's usual way of acting.
*During the first few weeks of the school year, we matched the incoming freshmen with seniors known for their nice **dispositions**.*

6. diverse (duh • vers') *adj.* Different; varied; dissimilar.
*Our school administrators want a **diverse** body of students, so they court students from all areas.*

7. dogma (dog' muh) *n*. Belief; tenet; doctrine.
*In my philosophy course at college, we examine the **dogma** of each philosopher.*

8. furtive (fur' tiv) *adj*. Sneaky; acting in a manner so as not to be observed; secret.
*When Megan acted in a **furtive** manner, we wondered what she was trying to hide.*

9. heterogeneous (het • ur • uh • jē' nē • us) *adj*. Consisting of different ingredients or unlike things; mixed.
*Most of the other students in my classes come from **heterogeneous** backgrounds, with different abilities and interests.*

10. homogeneous (hō • muh • je' nē • us) *adj*. Being the same throughout; being uniform.
*Even if a group of students appears to be **homogeneous**, they are actually not the same at all.*

Practices

PRACTICE A

Directions: Define the following words.

1. Animate _____

2. Animus _____

3. Depose _____

4. Dictum _____

5. Disposition _____

6. Diverse _____

7. Dogma _____

8. Furtive _____

9. Heterogeneous _____

10. Homogeneous _____

STOP. *Check answers at the back of the book on page 249.*

PRACTICE B

Directions: Match the meaning with the word from the word list.

WORD LIST

animate	animus	depose	dictum	disposition
diverse	dogma	furtive	heterogeneous	homogeneous

1. Secret _____

2. Mixed _____

3. Lively _____

4. Dissimilar _____

5. Belief _____

6. Saying _____

7. A natural tendency _____

8. Hatred _____

9. To remove _____

10. Being the same throughout _____

> **STOP.** *Check answers at the back of the book on page 249.*

PRACTICE C

Directions: Choose the word from the word list that *best* fits in the blank. Some blanks can be filled with more than one word. If necessary, you may change the form of the word in the word list.

WORD LIST

animate	animus	depose	dictum	disposition
diverse	dogma	furtive	heterogeneous	homogeneous

1. The officers of our school organizations told the college administrators that their members had a(n) _____ of nonviolent demonstrations.

2. We decided that for the good of our school, we had to _____ the leader of the group that destroyed school property.

3. As she has such a delightful _____, I'm sure she will be happy to help you.

4. It was hard for Maria not to feel _____ for the people who murdered her brother.

5. My class is made up of a (n) _____ group of students.

6. We began to suspect something when Jake behaved in such a(n) _____ manner because he was usually very open about everything.

7. _____ grouping, that is, grouping students according to similarities, is quite difficult.

8. Most classes are _____ grouped.

9. I have a certain basic _____, but lately, I keep changing it based on which professor I have.

10. My teacher's usually unexpressive face becomes _____ when she reads aloud a poem she loves.

LESSON 38

WORDS

bellicose	egregious	erratic	germane	hyperbole
obdurate	paternalism	periphery	Pollyanna	poltergeist

1. **bellicose** (bel′ uh • kōs) *adj.* Eager to fight; warlike; belligerent; quarrelsome.
   *My friends and I avoid **bellicose** people because we are very peaceful.*

2. **egregious** (ē • grē′ jus) *adj.* Outstanding for undesirable qualities; bad.
   *I could not believe that I had made such an **egregious** error on my term paper.*

3. **erratic** (ir • at′ ik) *adj.* Wandering; not regular; not stable.
   *His behavior had become so **erratic** that we wondered if he was mentally stable.*

4. **germane** (gur • mān′) *adj.* Relevant; to the point; pertinent.
   *What he had to say on the issue was certainly **germane**.*

5. **hyperbole** (hī • per′ buh • lē) *n.* Gross exaggeration or overstatement.
   *When Peter said that he had eaten 100 pancakes, we knew that he was resorting to **hyperbole**.*

6. **obdurate** (ob′ door • it) *adj.* Not easily moved to pity or sympathy; hard-hearted; not giving in readily; stubborn; inflexible.
   *Our **obdurate** instructor said that the date for the final was set and she could not do anything about changing it.*

7. **paternalism** (puh • ter′ nul • iz • um) *adj.* The principle or system of governing or controlling a nation, a group of people, and so forth in a manner similar to a father's relationship with his children.
   *The members of the administration at our college behave with such **paternalism** toward us that they must think of us as children.*

8. **periphery** (puh • rif′ur • ēe) *n.* A boundary line, especially of a rounded figure; perimeter; an outside surface, especially of a rounded figure.
   *Our college has beautiful shrubs at the **periphery** of its property.*

9. **Pollyanna** (pol • ē • an′ uh) *n.* Name of the young heroine of Eleanor Porter's novels; an excessively optimistic person.

*At school, we called Bethany Ms. **Pollyanna** because she always looked on the bright side of things.*

10. **poltergeist** (pol′ tur • gīst) *n.* A ghost supposed to be responsible for mysterious noisy disturbances.

*In the movie, there is a **poltergeist** in the house that mysteriously moves things and frightens the occupants.*

Practices

PRACTICE A

Directions: Define the following words.

1. Bellicose _____

2. Egregious _____

3. Erratic _____

4. Germane _____

5. Hyperbole _____

6. Obdurate _____

7. Paternalism _____

8. Periphery _____

9. Pollyanna _____

10. Poltergeist _____

STOP. *Check answers at the back of the book on page 249.*

PRACTICE B

Directions: Match the meaning with the word from the word list.

WORD LIST

bellicose	egregious	erratic	germane	hyperbole
obdurate	paternalism	periphery	Pollyanna	poltergeist

1. A person who always is optimistic _____

2. Warlike _____

3. A boundary _____

4. Wandering _____

5. Exceedingly bad _____

6. Gross exaggeration _____

7. Stubborn _____

8. A ghost that makes mysterious noises _____

9. Relevant _____

10. Someone who governs as a father _____

> **STOP.** *Check answers at the back of the book on page 249.*

PRACTICE C

Directions: Choose the word from the word list that *best* fits in the blank. A word may be used once only. If necessary, you may change the form of the word in the word list.

WORD LIST

bellicose	egregious	erratic	germane	hyperbole
obdurate	paternalism	periphery	Pollyanna	poltergeist

1. Did you see the scary movie called _____, in which a child gets trapped in a television set?

2. Some high-level corporation heads act in a(n) _____ way toward their employees.

3. That was an exceedingly _____ error that she made.

4. The words belligerent and _____ share a similar meaning.

5. The driver was driving in such a(n) _____ way that we assumed he was drunk.

6. If something is _____ to something else, it is relevant to it.

7. The words _____ and stubborn are synonyms.

8. When someone says, "I can eat everything in sight by myself," he or she is using _____.

9. The words perimeter and _____ are synonyms.

10. When a person always looks at the bright side of things, we usually call her Miss _____.

LESSON 39

WORDS

euthanasia	flagrant	magnate	perfidious	plausible
psychic	psychopath	sedition	sophistry	stipend

1. **euthanasia** (ū • thuh • nā′ zhuh) *n.* Act of causing a painless death, advocated by some to deal with those dying from an incurable disease.
   *In many states in this country, it is against the law to practice **euthanasia**.*

2. **flagrant** (flā′ grunt) *adj.* Glaringly bad; outrageous; notorious.
   *My roommate's taste in clothes is so **flagrant** that I am often embarrassed to be seen with her.*

3. **magnate** (mag′ nāt) *n.* A very important or influential person.
   *A billionaire would probably be called a **magnate**.*

4. **perfidious** (pur • fid′ ē • us) *adj.* Violating good trust; treacherous; deceitful; deliberately faithless.
   *I did not know I had a **perfidious** person as my friend until I learned that he had told all my secrets to others.*

5. **plausible** (plaw′ zuh • bul) *adj.* Acceptable; seemingly true; seemingly honest, trustworthy.
   *Her argument was quite **plausible**, so we believed her.*

6. **psychic** (sī′ kik) *n.* A person who is supposedly sensitive to the forces beyond the physical world; a medium. *adj.* Having to do with the mind; sensitive to forces beyond the physical world.
   *I could not believe that my roommate went to a **psychic** when his best buddy died.*

7. **psychopath** (sī′ kō • path) *n.* A person suffering from a mental disorder.
   *When one of our roommates started to rant and rave, we feared that he might be a **psychopath**.*

8. **sedition** (suh • dish′ un) *n.* The stirring up of discontent; resistance or rebellion against the government in power.

*It is considered a crime to advocate **sedition,** whereby people try to stir up others to overthrow the government.*

9. **sophistry** (sof′ ist • rē) *n.* Faulty reasoning; unsound or misleading but clever and appearing real argument or reasoning.

*Some people are so clever in presenting their illogical arguments that it is difficult to recognize that their arguments are filled with **sophistry.***

10. **stipend** (stī′ pund) *n.* A regular payment for services rendered; a wage.

*In our agreement, we said that we wanted a specific **stipend.***

Practices

PRACTICE A

Directions: Define the following words.

1. Euthanasia _____

2. Flagrant _____

3. Magnate _____

4. Perfidious _____

5. Plausible _____

6. Psychic _____

7. Psychopath _____

8. Sedition _____

9. Sophistry _____

10. Stipend _____

> **STOP.** *Check answers at the back of the book on page 249.*

PRACTICE B

Directions: Fill in the blank with the word from the word list.

WORD LIST

euthanasia	flagrant	magnate	perfidious	plausible
psychic	psychopath	sedition	sophistry	stipend

1. Faulty reasoning _____

2. Exceedingly bad _____

3. A person who is sensitive to forces beyond the physical world _____

4. Not trustworthy _____

5. Acceptable _____

6. A person suffering from a mental illness _____

7. An act causing a painless death _____

8. An influential person _____

9. A wage _____

10. To stir up discontent against a government in power _____

STOP. *Check answers at the back of the book on page 249.*

PRACTICE C

Directions: Choose the word from the word list that best fits in the blank. A word may be used once only. If necessary, you may change the form of the word in the word list.

WORD LIST

| euthanasia | flagrant | magnate | perfidious | plausible |
| psychic | psychopath | sedition | sophistry | stipend |

1. Last year I had a broker in another investment firm who made a(n) _____ error in my account.

2. I have known some people who begged others to help them commit _____.

3. When a well-known _____ who is very wealthy lost his money, he tried to kill himself.

4. It just does not seem _____ to me that someone would try to end his own life over money.

5. Perhaps a(n) _____ would try to take his life, but I cannot imagine a "normal" person doing that.

6. During Greek times, sophists were known for _____.

7. My mother went to a(n) _____ to see if the person could actually help her communicate with my dead father.

8. If you are going to entrust lots of money to someone, you want a trustworthy person, not a(n) _____ one.

9. In the United States, it is a crime to commit _____ against the government.

10. Many retired people receive certain _____ that allows them to quit their jobs.

Multiple-Choice Assessment of Lessons 37–39

Directions: Words are arranged by lesson. Underline the meaning that *best* fits the word. Answers are at the end of the book. **If you miss any word meaning, go back to the lesson and restudy the word.**

LESSON 37

1. animate
   a. refers to animals
   b. to make alive
   c. to amuse
   d. actors

2. animus
   a. to make alive
   b. to like someone
   c. to hibernate
   d. hatred

3. depose
   a. to let fall
   b. to cut off one's head
   c. to put on a throne
   d. to drop

4. dictum
   a. what politicians say
   b. someone's natural tendency
   c. a saying
   d. a tendency

5. disposition
   a. refers to a mind
   b. refers to a frame
   c. one's mind
   d. one's usual frame of mind

6. diverse
   a. different
   b. refers to many
   c. more than one
   d. refers to race

7. dogma
   a. a belief
   b. a special saying
   c. others' beliefs
   d. refers to one's mind

8. furtive
   a. trying to be observed
   b. trying to act like an animal
   c. trying to be funny
   d. secret

9. heterogeneous
   a. being the same throughout
   b. consisting of similar items
   c. being different throughout
   d. being uniform

10. homogeneous
   a. mixed
   b. refers to uniforms
   c. being the same throughout
   d. secret

LESSON 38

11. bellicose
   a. war
   b. strange
   c. warlike
   d. afraid

12. egregious
   a. outstanding
   b. quality
   c. bad
   d. afraid

13. erratic
   a. a wanderer
   b. not stable
   c. stable
   d. regular

14. germane
   a. relevant
   b. regular
   c. stable
   d. not pertinent

15. hyperbole
   a. gross
   b. overstatement
   c. exaggeration
   d. not stable

16. obdurate
   a. hard
   b. easily moved
   c. sympathetic
   d. stubborn

17. paternalism
   a. a father
   b. governing similar to a father
   c. relates to a father
   d. a father's relationship to his
      children

18. periphery
   a. a line
   b. the end
   c. a boundary line
   d. a rounded figure

19. Pollyanna
   a. a female
   b. an optimist
   c. a famous female
   d. a pessimist

20. poltergeist
   a. a friendly spirit
   b. a friendly ghost
   c. a responsible ghost
   d. a supposed noisy ghost

LESSON 39

21. euthanasia
   a. assistance
   b. causing a painless death
   c. death
   d. murder

22. flagrant
   a. very bad
   b. something good
   c. a flogging
   d. refers to a famous person

23. **magnate**
    a. a man
    b. refers to magnets
    c. a magician
    d. an influential person

24. **perfidious**
    a. trusting
    b. trustworthy
    c. deceitful
    d. not a liar

25. **plausible**
    a. seemingly untrue
    b. unacceptable
    c. seemingly true
    d. regular

26. **psychic**
    a. a sensitive person
    b. a person
    c. an unusual person
    d. a medium

27. **psychopath**
    a. an unusual person
    b. a person with a mental problem
    c. someone in an asylum
    d. a sensitive person

28. **sedition**
    a. a crime
    b. a law
    c. stirring up discontent against government
    d. a rebellious person

29. **sophistry**
    a. someone who lies
    b. faulty reasoning
    c. reasoning
    d. a believer

30. **stipend**
    a. a wage
    b. to make a specific demand
    c. to write a contract
    d. an agreement

STOP. *Check answers at the back of the book on page 249.*

LESSON 40

WORDS

bibliophile	bibliotherapy	collate	condone	euphonious
euphoria	genocide	veracity	verbatim	voracious

1. **bibliophile** (bib′ lē • uh • fīl) *n.* A person who loves books; a collector of books.
   *We decided that our English teacher is a **bibliophile** because she is always talking about how she loves books.*

2. **bibliotherapy** (bib′ lē • uh • ther • uh • pē) *n.* The use of books to help people deal with their emotional and adjustment problems; books used as guidance.
   *When the teacher learned that many of her students had divorced parents, she decided to use **bibliotherapy** to help these children.*

3. **collate** (kuh • lāt′) or (kō • lāt′) *v.* To gather together a text, book, papers, and so forth in proper order; to compare critically to note similarities or differences.
   *Our instructor wanted us to **collate** our report.*

4. **condone** (kon • dōn′) *v.* To overlook, forgive, or pardon an offense.
   *We decided to **condone** her offense because she seemed genuinely sorry.*

5. **euphonious** (ū • fō′ nē • us) *adj.* Harmonious; having a pleasant sound.
   *Mike said that he loves to hear Jennifer speak because her voice is so **euphonious**.*

6. **euphoria** (ū • for′ ē • uh) *n.* A feeling of high spirits, vigor, or well-being.
   *Carol was in a state of **euphoria** when she heard that she had just won the lottery.*

7. **genocide** (jen′ uh • sīd) *n.* The systematic and deliberate killing of a whole racial, ethnic, or religious group of people bound together by customs, language, politics, and so on.
   *In World War II, Hitler attempted to commit **genocide** against the Jewish people because he wanted to wipe them out completely.*

8. veracity (vuh • ras′ uh • tē) *n.* Honesty; truthfulness.
*When José promised to tell the truth and nothing but the truth, we believed him because he always spoke with **veracity**.*

9. verbatim (vur • bāt′ • um) *adv.* Following the original word for word; word for word; in exactly the same words.
*He repeated the message **verbatim**.*

10. voracious (vuh • rā′ shus) *adj.* Very greedy especially in eating; devouring lots of food; greedy in some desire or pursuit.
*When we invited Jim for dinner, we couldn't believe what a **voracious** appetite he had.*

Practices

PRACTICE A

Directions: Define the following words.

1. Bibliophile _____

2. Bibliotherapy _____

3. Collate _____

4. Condone _____

5. Euphonious _____

6. Euphoria _____

7. Genocide _____

8. Veracity _____

9. Verbatim _____

10. Voracious _____

> **STOP.** *Check answers at the back of the book on page 250.*

PRACTICE B

Directions: Match the meaning with the word from the word list.

WORD LIST

bibliophile	bibliotherapy	collate	condone	euphonious
euphoria	genocide	veracity	verbatim	voracious

1. Lover of books _____

2. Word for word _____

3. To forgive _____

4. Good sounding _____

5. To gather papers together in proper order _____

6. Truthfulness _____

7. Guidance using books _____

8. Greedy appetite _____

9. The killing of a whole group of people _____

10. A feeling of high spirits _____

STOP. *Check answers at the back of the book on page 250.*

PRACTICE C

Directions: Choose the word from the word list that *best* fits in the blank. A word may be used once only. If necessary, you may change the form of the word in the word list.

WORD LIST

| bibliophile | bibliotherapy | collate | condone | euphonious |
| euphoria | genocide | veracity | verbatim | voracious |

1. The word *cope* is an important one in relation to _____, which deals with the use of books as therapy.

2. My brother has quite a(n) _____ appetite.

3. Please speak slowly and tell me _____ the message she left.

4. I like to _____ my material so that it is in proper order.

5. You call a lover of books a(n) _____.

6. Megan said that she would _____ his mistake if he promised never to repeat it.

7. Mike was so happy when Megan forgave him that he went into a state of _____.

8. It doesn't seem possible that _____ still exists in the world.

9. It seems amazing that some people can look you right in the eye and claim that they are speaking with _____, yet they are being untruthful.

10. Some people's voices are so _____ that you love to hear them speak.

WORDS

consensus	deviant	diverge	obliterate	obsequious
philanderer	pristine	seduce	solecism	surrogate

1. **consensus** (kon • sen′ sus) *n.* An agreement held by all or almost all; general agreement, especially in opinion.
   *The **consensus** of our group was that we go on the boat ride.*

2. **deviant** (dē′ vē • unt) *adj.* Tending to turn from what is considered normal in a group or society.
   *No one should have to put up with such **deviant** behavior.*

3. **diverge** (dī • verj′) *v.* To move in different directions from a starting point; deviate; to take on gradually a different form or to become a different kind; to depart from a particular viewpoint.
   *We were surprised when our instructor **diverged** from his usual lecture and talked to us about our opinions about his course.*

4. **obliterate** (uh • blit′ ur • āt) *v.* Erase; to destroy; to leave no trace.
   *It was upsetting to see the wrecking crew **obliterate** our old house so that a highway could be built.*

5. **obsequious** (ub • sē′ kwē • us) *adj.* Fawning; showing too great a willingness to serve or obey.
   *It was annoying to have such an **obsequious** server watching us eat.*

6. **philanderer** (fi • lan′ dur • ur) *n.* A man who engages lightly in love affairs; a man who is insincere in his love of a woman.
   *We all felt that John was a **philanderer** because he would profess his love for whatever woman he was going with at the time, but he was very insincere about his feelings.*

7. pristine (pris' tēn) *adj.* Pure; uncorrupted; original; unspoiled; characteristic of the earliest period or condition.

*We were impressed by the **pristine** condition of the lake.*

8. seduce (suh • dūs') *v.* To persuade to do something that is disloyal or disobedient; to lure.

*John, who is a philanderer, tried to **seduce** one of his teachers so that he could get a good grade in her class.*

9. solecism (sol' uh • siz • um) *n.* A violation of the conventional usage of words; ungrammatical use of words.

*It is a **solecism** to say "We done that" instead of "We did that."*

10. surrogate (sur' uh • gāt) *n.* A substitute; a person of some authority who replaces a mother or father in one's feelings.

*In one of our science experiments, the monkey used a blanket as a **surrogate** for her mother.*

Practices

PRACTICE A

Directions: Define the following words.

1. Consensus _____

2. Deviant _____

3. Diverge _____

4. Obliterate _____

5. Obsequious _____

6. Philanderer _____

7. Pristine _____

8. Seduce _____

9. Solecism _____

10. Surrogate _____

STOP. *Check answers at the back of the book on page 250.*

PRACTICE B

Directions: Match the meaning with the word from the word list.

WORD LIST

consensus	deviant	diverge	obliterate	obsequious
philanderer	pristine	seduce	solecism	surrogate

1. Ungrammatical use of a word _____

2. To persuade to do something _____

3. General agreement _____

4. To leave no trace _____

5. Uncorrupted _____

6. A substitute _____

7. Fawning _____

8. Tending to move from the norm in a group _____

9. To move in different directions from a starting point _____

10. A man who engages lightly in love affairs _____

STOP. *Check answers at the back of the book on page 250.*

PRACTICE C

Directions: Choose the word from the word list that *best* fits in the blank. A word may be used once only. If necessary, you may change the form of the word in the word list.

WORD LIST

consensus	deviant	diverge	obliterate	obsequious
philanderer	pristine	seduce	solecism	surrogate

1. In a democracy, we often try to get a(n) _____ of opinion before we start something new.

2. It really bothers me when someone behaves in a fawning or _____ manner.

3. The word _____ means "to destroy completely."

4. "When two paths _____, the one you take makes all the difference," wrote poet Robert Frost in a well-known poem.

5. In some experiments with monkeys, a blanket can become a(n) _____ mother.

6. It's a(n) _____ to say "I is going to town" instead of "I am going to town."

7. Our instructor told us to be careful not to be _____ by the simple language used in the textbook, because the material it covers is actually very difficult.

8. Mary said that she enjoyed the _____ forest because it seemed untouched by humans.

9. Unfortunately, Robyn learned that she was married to a(n) _____ who liked to fool around with lots of women.

10. Robyn divorced her husband because she felt that his behavior was _____.

WORDS

angst	assimilate	aversion	dichotomy	fluent
pivotal	plateau	plenary	pundit	relent

1. **angst** (angst) *n.* Anxiety; a gloomy feeling of depression.
   *When Jessica arrived at college as a freshman, she had lots of **angst** about almost everything.*

2. **assimilate** (uh • sim′ uh • lāt) *v.* To absorb into one's thinking; to change food into a form that can be absorbed by the body; to make like or alike.
   *In our science class, we learned about how the body **assimilates** food.*

3. **aversion** (uh • ver′ shun) *n.* An intense dislike.
   *Megan said that she had an **aversion** to meat.*

4. **dichotomy** (di • kot′ uh • mē) *n.* Division into two parts, groups, or classes, especially when these are sharply distinguished or opposed.
   *It is a **dichotomy** when you want to both stay and go but you cannot make up your mind about what to do.*

5. **fluent** (flū′ unt) *adj.* Able to speak and write easily; flowing or moving smoothly.
   *My best friend is **fluent** in Spanish and French.*

6. **pivotal** (piv′ uh • tul) *adj.* Acting as a pivot, that is, acting as the person or thing around which something turns or depends; central; crucial; critical.
   *Lisa knew that she was **pivotal** to our plan being a success.*

7. **plateau** (plat′ ō) *n.* A period or level of relative stability; an elevated tract of almost level land; a level in which a person's learning rate does not increase.

*Frances said that she had reached a **plateau** in playing the violin and was no longer improving her ability.*

8. **plenary** (plē′ nuh • rē) *adj.* Full; complete; absolute; refers to attendance by all members.

*When we have a **plenary** session of our club, we expect all members to attend.*

9. **pundit** (pun′ dit) *n.* A person who is very knowledgeable or claims to have great learning.

*There are many **pundits** on television talk shows who seem to be knowledgeable of whatever topic is being discussed.*

10. **relent** (ri • lent′) *v.* To yield or give in; to become less severe, stern, or stubborn

*Jim complained so much about the work load that our teaching assistant finally decided to **relent** and change our exam date.*

Practices

PRACTICE A

Directions: Define the following words.

1. Angst _____

2. Assimilate _____

3. Aversion _____

4. Dichotomy _____

5. Fluent _____

6. Pivotal _____

7. Plateau _____

8. Plenary _____

9. Pundit _____

10. Relent _____

STOP. *Check answers at the back of the book on page 250.*

PRACTICE B

Directions: Match the meaning with the word from the word list.

WORD LIST

angst	assimilate	aversion	dichotomy	fluent
pivotal	plateau	plenary	pundit	relent

1. Strong dislike _____

2. Central _____

3. Full _____

4. Someone regarded as knowledgeable _____

5. To yield _____

6. Able to communicate well in speech or writing _____

7. Anxiety _____

8. A flat tract of land _____

9. Division into two parts _____

10. To absorb into one's thinking _____

STOP. *Check answers at the back of the book on page 250.*

PRACTICE C

Directions: Choose the word from the word list that *best* fits in the blank. A word may be used once only. If necessary, you may change the form of the word in the word list.

WORD LIST

angst	assimilate	aversion	dichotomy	fluent
pivotal	plateau	plenary	pundit	relent

1. Matt had a severe _____ to Brad, so he didn't want to room with him.

2. Matt felt great _____ because he was concerned about who his roommate would be.

3. Matt is _____ in several languages, so he was hoping his roommate would be able to speak another language besides English.

4. Actually, Matt felt that he had hit a(n) _____ in relation to developing his foreign language ability.

5. Matt feels that to _____ to another culture, it is important to learn the language of its people.

6. Matt seemed to feel that getting a roommate to whom he could relate was _____ to his success at school.

7. Matt always felt that he was in a(n) _____ because he always seemed to want to do two things at once.

8. Many television stations have a(n) _____ who everyone regards as knowledgeable.

9. To decide who would represent our class, we had a (n) _____ meeting.

10. I hate meetings where no one will _____ or yield to another person.

Multiple-Choice Assessment of Lessons 40–42

Directions: Words are arranged by lesson. Underline the meaning that *best* fits the word. Answers are at the end of the book. **If you miss any word meaning, go back to the lesson and restudy the word.**

LESSON 40

1. bibliophile
   a. lover
   b. lover of books
   c. refers to books
   d. hater of books

2. bibliotherapy
   a. refers to therapy
   b. lover of books
   c. guidance using books
   d. refers to books

3. collate
   a. to gather together
   b. to gather together a paper
   c. to work with papers
   d. to gather together a paper in proper order

4. condone
   a. to punish
   b. to find guilt
   c. to acquit
   d. to forgive

5. euphonious
   a. refers to sounds
   b. refers to something noisy
   c. having a pleasant sound
   d. refers to feeling well

6. euphoria
   a. high
   b. a feeling of well-being
   c. refers to spirits
   d. a feeling

7. genocide
   a. refers to killing
   b. the killing of a whole group
      of people
   c. refers to race
   d. a people bound together

8. veracity
   a. honesty
   b. refers to a city
   c. refers to telling
      the truth
   d. a big appetite

9. verbatim
   a. truthfulness
   b. refers to truth
   c. word for word
   d. honesty

10. voracious
   a. very big
   b. telling the truth
   c. very greedy
   d. refers to eating

LESSON 41

11. consensus
   a. an agreement
   b. an agreement by all
   c. exact opinion
   d. refers to everyone

12. deviant
   a. tending to be normal
   b. turning away
   c. tending to turn from what is
      normal
   d. refers to a normal society

13. diverge
   a. deviate
   b. to move away
   c. tending to turn
   d. to leave

14. obliterate
   a. erase
   b. to be literate
   c. to decimate
   d. to write

15. obsequious
   a. to be a pest
   b. refers to servers
   c. fawning
   d. refers to eating

16. philanderer
   a. a criminal
   b. refers to a man
   c. a light love affair
   d. an insincere man in affairs of
      the heart

17. pristine
   a. something spoiled
   b. pure
   c. something corrupted
   d. impure

18. seduce
   a. to become involved in a love
      affair
   b. to love
   c. refers to love affairs
   d. to lure

19. solecism
   a. refers to grammar
   b. unconventional
   c. conventional use of words
   d. ungrammatical use of words

20. surrogate
   a. replacement therapy
   b. refers to mother
   c. a substitute
   d. refers to parents

LESSON 42

21. angst
- a. a problem
- b. anxiety
- c. to depress
- d. fearful of another

22. assimilate
- a. gather
- b. to make
- c. absorption
- d. to make part of one's thinking

23. aversion
- a. dislike
- b. to change
- c. division
- d. intense

24. dichotomy
- a. two things
- b. a division
- c. division into two
- d. something opposed

25. fluent
- a. smooth person
- b. able to do things
- c. able to move well
- d. speak easily

26. pivotal
- a. refers to turning
- b. central
- c. refers to a stable
- d. turning around

27. plateau
- a. flat tire
- b. relative stable period
- c. something flat
- d. a period of time

28. plenary
- a. refers to sessions
- b. complete
- c. refers to attendance
- d. refers to members

29. pundit
- a. refers to a person
- b. someone knowledgeable
- c. someone on TV
- d. refers to talk shows

30. relent
- a. give in
- b. to try
- c. to become severe
- d. to relate to others

STOP. Check answers at the back of the book on page 250.

LESSON 43

WORDS

abyss	adversity	corpulent	discourse	epiphany
expediency	fortify	graphic	introvert	subtle

1. **abyss** (uh • bis′) *n.* A bottomless gulf; a deep crack in the earth; anything too deep to be measured; profound depth.
   *She was astounded at the **abyss** that the earthquake had made.*

2. **adversity** (ad • vur′ suh • tē) *n.* A state of being in trouble; a state of wretchedness or misfortune.
   *Some lawyers seem to prosper in times of **adversity**.*

3. **corpulent** (kor′ pū • lunt) *adj.* Fat and fleshy; obese.
   *It is not politically correct to call someone fat or obese; the more acceptable word is **corpulent**.*

4. **discourse** (dis′ kors) *n.* A long and formal treatment of a subject in speech or writing; a lecture or dissertation; communication of ideas, especially in speech or writing; conversation.
   *Our instructor tends to give a long **discourse** on his favorite topic.*

5. **epiphany** (ē • pif′ uh • nē) *n.* A revelation; a sudden flash of insight.
   *Have you ever had an **epiphany,** where suddenly everything becomes clear to you?*

6. **expediency** (ek • spē′ dē • un • sē) *n.* The quality of being useful for effecting a desired result; appropriateness to the conditions; self-interest; the doing of what is of selfish use rather than what is right or just.
   *It seemed that Cliff acted with **expediency** rather than doing what was right or just.*

7. **fortify** (fort′ uh • fī) *v.* Make strong or stronger; to strengthen against attack; to support a statement; to corroborate.
   *The speaker said that he would **fortify** his statement with lots of research.*

8. **graphic** (graf′ ik) *adj.* Marked by realistic and marked detail.
   *My roommate's description of her attacker on campus was so **graphic** that the police artist had no trouble drawing a good rendering of him.*

9. **introvert** (in′ tro • vurt) *n.* One whose interests are mostly concerned with him- or herself rather than to external objects or people.
   *Some people may think that an **introvert** is stuck on him- or herself, but the person may just be shy.*

10. **subtle** (sut′ ul) *adj.* Something thin—not dense; delicately skillful or clever; not open or direct; crafty; sly; delicately suggestive—not greatly obvious.
    *My college roommate would not come out and say that she disliked someone, but her **subtle** behavior toward the person made her feelings clear.*

Practices

PRACTICE A

Directions: Match the meaning with the word from the word list.

WORD LIST

abyss	adversity	corpulent	discourse	epiphany
expediency	fortify	graphic	introvert	subtle

1. It wasn't until George had finished speaking that I had a sudden _____ about what he was trying to say.

2. In life, we seem to have to overcome lots of _____.

3. Mike prefers to use a euphemism for the word *fat*, so he uses the word _____ to describe his opponent.

4. She needed to act with great _____ to overcome her opponent.

5. When her opponent started to attack her arguments in the case, Sharon gave a(n) _____ description of the murderer that left nothing to the imagination.

6. The _____ that Sharon had made in her opponent's argument was too deep to overcome.

7. When Jennifer was preparing her summation to the jury as to why her client was innocent, she remembered a lecture, that is, a(n) _____ her professor had once given on the subject.

8. There's no question that Jennifer's client is a(n) _____ because he is so focused on his own thoughts.

9. Jennifer knew that she had to be direct and not _____ when she presented her summation to the jury.

10. Jennifer knew that she needed to use lots of research to _____ her summation.

STOP. *Check answers at the back of the book on page 250.*

PRACTICE B

Directions: Define the following words.

1. Abyss _____

2. Adversity _____

3. Corpulent _____

4. Discourse _____

5. Epiphany _____

6. Expediency _____

7. Fortify _____

8. Graphic _____

9. Introvert _____

10. Subtle _____

STOP. *Check answers at the back of the book on page 250.*

PRACTICE C

Directions: Match the number of the word in Column A with the letter of its meaning in Column B.

	Column A	Column B
_____	1. abyss	a. fat and fleshy
_____	2. adversity	b. make strong
_____	3. corpulent	c not open or direct
_____	4. discourse	d. self-interest
_____	5. epiphany	e. concerned primarily with one's own thoughts
_____	6. expediency	f. marked by realistic detail
_____	7. fortify	g. a revelation
_____	8. graphic	h. a bottomless gulf
_____	9. introvert	i. a state of being in trouble
_____	10. subtle	j. communication of ideas

LESSON 44

bilateral	binary	definitive	fluctuate	gratuitous
marathon	morose	mortify	prerequisite	remnant

1. **bilateral** (bī • lat′ uh • rul) *adj.* Involving two sides.
   *The two nations began **bilateral** talks, hoping to conclude a peace treaty between them.*

2. **binary** (bī′ nuh • rē) *adj.* Twofold; made up of two parts; relating to base two.
   *The **binary** system of numbers is used with digital computers.*

3. **definitive** (di • fin′ uh • tiv) *adj.* Conclusive, final; most nearly complete or accurate
   *The results of the study are not **definitive** because they contain too many different conclusions.*

4. **fluctuate** (fluk′ chu • āt) *v.* To be continually changing or varying.
   *It's hard to know what Jack really thinks when his views keep **fluctuating**.*

5. **gratuitous** (gra • tōo′ i • tus) *adj.* Granted without obligation; given without any charge; free; given without any justification.
   *We could not believe our luck when we were told that our stay at the resort was a **gratuitous** gesture on someone's part, so we didn't have to pay anything.*

6. **marathon** (mar′ uh • than) *n.* Any long-distance or endurance race.
   *At college, we often participated in a special bicycle **marathon** to determine who had the greatest amount of endurance.*

7. **morose** (muh • rōs′) *adj.* Gloomy, sullen; ill-tempered.
   *Whenever it is a dark and gloomy day outside, our buddy becomes particularly **morose**.*

8. **mortify** (mor′ tuh • fī) *v.* To cause to feel shame; to cause to feel humiliation. To punish (one's body) or to control (one's physical desires or pas-

sions) by self-denial, fasting, and the like as a means of religious or severe discipline.

*We were all **mortified** that our buddies were involved in a fight that caused so many people to get hurt.*

9. **prerequisite** (pre • rek′ wuh • zit) *adj.* Something required beforehand; a necessary condition for something following.

*At our school, there are many **prerequisite** courses you must take before you can take certain courses in your major.*

10. **remnant** (rem′ nunt) *n.* Remainder; what is left over. A small remaining part, quantity, or number of people or things; a trace, last remaining indication of what has been.

*I needed more cloth to finish sewing my formal, but all I had left was a **remnant**.*

Practices

PRACTICE A

Directions: Choose a word from the word list that *best* fits the blank in each sentence.

WORD LIST

bilateral	binary	definitive	fluctuate	gratuitous
marathon	morose	mortify	prerequisite	remnant

1. When children start school, they usually have a dominant side, but some children are still _____

2. Our minister said that he would try not to _____ us by his sermon.

3. In the summer, some television channels hold a (n) _____ of a TV series; for example, the station begins showing episodes of the show in the morning and continues showing them until midnight.

4. They _____ from being good guys and bad guys, based on their mood.

5. Why are you so sad? You look _____ today.

6. I need more than a small _____ of material to finish what I am sewing.

7. Because we helped José, he treated us to a(n) _____ meal.

8. Digital computers use the _____ system.

9. A reading course is usually a(n) _____ for the diagnosis course at our school.

10. The instructor told her students to make sure the results of their research were conclusive, that is, were _____.

STOP. *Check answers at the back of the book on page 250.*

PRACTICE B

Directions: Define the following words.

1. Bilateral _____

2. Binary _____

3. Definitive_____

4. Fluctuate _____

5. Gratuitous _____

6. Marathon _____

7. Morose _____

8. Mortify _____

9. Prerequisite _____

10. Remnant _____

STOP. *Check answers at the back of the book on page 250.*

PRACTICE C

Directions: Match the number of the word in Column A with the letter of its meaning in Column B.

	Column A	*Column B*
_____	1. bilateral	a. gloomy
_____	2. binary	b. any long-distance or endurance race
_____	3. definitive	c. two-sided
_____	4. fluctuate	d. final
_____	5. gratuitous	e. to cause to feel shame
_____	6. marathon	f. free

_____ 7. morose

_____ 8. mortify

_____ 9. prerequisite

_____ 10. remnant

g. relating to base two

h. to be continually changing

i. remainder

j. something required beforehand

STOP. *Check answers at the back of the book on page 250.*

LESSON 45

WORDS

acrid	ameliorate	annuity	automaton	autonomous
biennial	bilingual	biopsy	contrite	podiatrist

1. **acrid** (ak′rid) *adj.* Sharp, bitter, stinging or irritating to the taste or smell; bitter or sarcastic in speech.

   *We couldn't believe how **acrid** Jason's speech was after he had lost the election.*

2. **ameliorate** (uh • mel′ yuh • rāt) *v.* To make or become better; to improve.

   *After Jason's speech, anything that he could say would have to **ameliorate** the situation.*

3. **annuity** (uh • nū′ uh • tē) *n.* An investment yielding a fixed sum of money payable yearly, to continue for a given number of years or for life; a yearly payment of money.

   *Since she began receiving a rather sizable **annuity** each year, she decided to retire at an early age.*

4. **automaton** (aw • tom′ uh • ton) *n.* Anything that can move or act by itself; a person or animal acting in an automatic or mechanical way.

   *The goose-stepping soldiers in Hitler's army looked like **automatons**.*

5. **autonomous** (aw • ton′ uh • mus) *adj.* Functioning independently of other parts; self-governing.

   *Each state is actually **autonomous** in the area of education because education is not mentioned in the United States Constitution.*

6. **biennial** (bī • en′ ē • ul) *adj.* Occurring once every two years; lasting for two years.

   *Because we can only afford a vacation every two years, it has become a **biennial** event.*

7. **bilingual** (bī • ling′ gwul) *adj.* Able to use two languages well.

   *In **bilingual** programs, students who speak a language other than English learn certain subjects in their native language.*

8. **biopsy** (bī′ op • se) *n.* In medicine, the cutting out of a piece of living tissue for examination.

   *To determine whether major surgery is necessary, the doctor usually takes a **biopsy** of the organ in question.*

9. **contrite** (kon′ trīt) *adj.* Feeling sorry or remorse for having done something wrong; showing remorse.

   *Ben said that he was **contrite** about having made such acrid remarks about his opponent.*

10. **podiatrist** (puh • dī′ uh • trist) *n.* A foot doctor; one who specializes in the care and treatment of the feet, especially foot disorders.

    *After I went on a ten-mile walk, my feet hurt so much that I needed to go see a **podiatrist**.*

Practices

PRACTICE A

Directions: Choose a word from the word list that *best* fits the blank in each sentence.

WORD LIST

acrid	ameliorate	annuity	automaton	autonomous
biennial	bilingual	biopsy	contrite	podiatrist

1. The judge said that he was giving Megan the maximum penalty because throughout her trial, she was not _____ about her actions.

2. We couldn't believe the _____ remarks that Belinda made about her roommate.

3. The _____ ruler felt that he could get away with anything.

4. Our picnic at the company for which we work has always been a(n) _____ event rather than an annual one.

5. Joel acts like a(n) _____ or like a machine.

6. Proponents of _____ education said that they wanted their children to learn the subjects in their native language even though they were in the United States.

7. My mother's _____ has allowed her to continue living after her retirement the way she had been before it.

8. Jesse went to a(n) _____ when she had an ingrown toenail.

9. The surgeon said that he needed to take a(n) _____ of one of Javaria's organs to determine if she needed extensive surgery.

10. At the time, it seemed that nothing anyone could do would _____ the situation between the two warring nations.

> **STOP.** *Check answers at the end of the book on page 250.*

PRACTICE B

Directions: Define the following words.

1. Acrid _____

2. Ameliorate _____

3. Annuity _____

4. Automaton _____

5. Autonomous _____

6. Biennial _____

7. Bilingual _____

8. Biopsy _____

9. Contrite _____

10. Podiatrist _____

> **STOP.** *Check answers at the end of the book on page 250.*

PRACTICE C

Directions: Match the word in Column A with its meaning in Column B.

	Column A	*Column B*
_____	1. acrid	a. to improve
_____	2. ameliorate	b. able to use two languages well
_____	3. annuity	c. lasting for two years
_____	4. automaton	d. anything that can move by itself
_____	5. autonomous	e. sharp

_____	6. biennial	f. self-governing
_____	7. bilingual	g. a foot doctor
_____	8. biopsy	h. showing remorse
_____	9. contrite	i. the cutting of human tissue for examination
_____	10. podiatrist	j. a yearly payment of money

Multiple-Choice Assessment of Lessons 43–45

Directions: Words are arranged by lesson. Underline the meaning that *best* fits the word. Answers are at the end of the book. **If you miss any word meaning, go back to the lesson and restudy the word.**

LESSON 43

1. abyss
a. a pit
b. a crack
c. a bottomless gulf
d. refers to the earth

2. adversity
a. refers to a state
b. a state of being
c. misfortune
d. a troublesome person

3. corpulent
a. very fleshy
b. a politically correct term
c. a euphemism
d. refers to the army corps

4. discourse
a. something formal
b. refers to what instructors do
c. a lecture
d. writing material

5. epiphany
a. refers to the Bible
b. a revelation
c. refers to a script
d. a sudden flash

6. expediency
a. selfish
b. self-interest
c. being useful
d. doing what is right

7. fortify
a. to hold
b. to support an attack
c. to attack
d. to strengthen

8. graphic
a. refers to graphs
b. refers to something pretty
c. descriptive
d. refers to something good

9. introvert
a. a person who looks inward
b. a person
c. one who looks outward
d. a relative

10. subtle
a. something dense
b. a crafty person
c. something direct
d. not greatly obvious

LESSON 44

11. bilateral
a. refers to sides
b. has to do with two sides
c. has to do with two
d. refers to peace treaties

12. binary
a. refers to two sides
b. refers to computers
c. base two
d. refers to bases

13. definitive
a. to skim
b. not conclusive
c. final
d. to try

14. fluctuate
a. to flow
b. to continue in a path
c. to grow
d. to continually change

15. gratuitous
a. pleasing
b. free
c. grateful
d. refers to tips

16. marathon
a. refers to TV shows
b. a race
c. strength
d. endurance race

17. morose
a. gloomy
b. refers to being silly
c. not smart
d. a moron

18. mortify
a. to cause to feel
b. refers to death
c. to cause shame
d. to be gloomy

19. prerequisite
a. refers to what follows
b. something required before
c. something required
d. something necessary after

20. remnant
a. remainder
b. something needed
c. refers to cloth
d. refers to material needed
   for sewing

LESSON 45

21. acrid
a. bitter taste or smell
b. refers to taste
c. refers to sound
d. refers to smell

22. ameliorate
a. to make bitter
b. to help
c. to improve
d. to speak

23. annuity
a. refers to yearly
b. refers to investment
c. refers to income
d. yearly payment of investment

24. automaton
a. mechanical toy
b. acting in a mechanical way
c. a machine
d. refers to a move

25. autonomous
   a. refers to oneself
   b. refers to functioning
   c. refers to oneself
   d. self-governing

26. biennial
   a. refers to two
   b. lasts forever
   c. lasts two years
   d. refers to years

27. bilingual
   a. refers to two
   b. using two languages equally well
   c. two languages
   d. refers to sides

28. biopsy
   a. refers to organs
   b. cutting of living tissue for examination
   c. refers to cutting
   d. an examination

29. contrite
   a. feeling sad
   b. feeling sorry for doing something wrong
   c. feeling gloomy
   d. refers to sorry

30. podiatrist
   a. foot doctor
   b. refers to feet
   c. refers to doctors
   d. refers to care

STOP. *Check answers at the back of the book on page 251.*

LESSON 46

WORDS

accreditation	disparity	endemic	exacerbate	microbe
phobia	purify	putrid	succinct	unison

1. **accreditation** (uh • kred′ i • tā • shun) *n.* A giving authority to; a vouching for; act of bringing into favor.
   *If a college does not have the proper **accreditation**, students graduating from it might have difficulty getting jobs or getting into graduate school.*

2. **disparity** (di • spar′ uh • tē) *n.* Unlikeness, inequality or difference.
   *The **disparity** between the two of us was obvious to everyone.*

3. **endemic** (en • dem′ ik) *adj.* Native to a particular place, usually said of plants, animals, and customs, and so on; constantly present in a particular region.
   *There are certain plants that are **endemic** to this region.*

4. **exacerbate** (eg • zas′ ur • bāt) *v.* To make more intense or sharp; to aggravate; to annoy, irritate, embitter.
   *There is no question that when Amy speaks, she **exacerbates** her audience.*

5. **microbe** (mī′ krōb) *n.* A very small living thing; a microorganism.
   *Doctors determine through tests what **microbes** in our bodies are causing our disease.*

6. **phobia** (fō′ bē • uh) *n.* Extreme fear.
   *My friend has such a severe **phobia** against cats that he is afraid to be in the same room with one.*

7. **purify** (pyur′ uh • fī) *v.* To rid of pollution; to free from guilt; to free from corrupt or incorrect elements; to purge.
   *At our school, the water was **purified** to make sure it was free of any pollutants.*

8. **putrid** (pū′ trid) *adj.* Rotten and foul-smelling; causing, showing, or proceeding from decay; morally corrupt; depraved.
   *The pond near our school was positively **putrid**.*

9. succinct (suk • sinkt′) *adj.* Terse; clearly and briefly stated; concise; to the point; brief.
*We told the after-dinner speaker to make his talk **succinct** if he wanted to keep his audience's attention.*

10. unison (ū′ nuh • son) *n.* A harmonious agreement; a saying of something together.
*Choral groups speak in **unison** when they recite.*

Practices

PRACTICE A

Directions: Choose a word from the word list that *best* fits the blank in each sentence.

WORD LIST

accreditation	disparity	endemic	exacerbate	microbe
phobia	purify	putrid	succinct	unison

1. Why do you have such a(n) _____ of cats?

2. There is a big _____ between Tawana and Josie when they play tennis.

3. Try to be _____ rather than verbose when making your after-dinner talk.

4. I think you will _____ the situation if you continue to act the way you are.

5. That plant is _____ to this region.

6. Has your college's business school received its _____?

7. A(n) _____ is so small that you need a high-powered microscope to see it.

8. We all sang in _____.

9. The smell at the mall was so _____ that it was closed until the source of the odor was discovered.

10. I hope that they _____ the water in my building; otherwise, I'm buying bottled water.

STOP. *Check answers at the back of the book on page 251.*

PRACTICE B

Directions: Define the following words.

1. Accreditation _____

2. Disparity _____

3. Endemic _____

4. Exacerbate _____

5. Microbe _____

6. Phobia _____

7. Purify _____

8. Putrid _____

9. Succinct _____

10. Unison _____

STOP. *Check answers at the back of the book on page 251.*

PRACTICE C

Directions: Match the number of the word in Column A to the letter of its meaning in Column B.

Column A	Column B
_____ 1. accreditation	a. unlikeness
_____ 2. disparity	b. a harmonious agreement
_____ 3. endemic	c. concise
_____ 4. exacerbate	d. a vouching for
_____ 5. microbe	e. to aggravate
_____ 6. phobia	f. native to a particular place
_____ 7. purify	g. extreme fear
_____ 8. putrid	h. to purge
_____ 9. succinct	i. a microorganism
_____ 10. unison	j. foul-smelling

47

WORDS

alias	alienate	anarchy	autocracy	creditor
demagogue	emigrate	monopoly	monotonous	speculate

1. **alias** (ā′ lē • us) *n.* Another name taken by a person, often a criminal.
   *People who use **aliases** don't want others to know their real names.*

2. **alienate** (āl′ yun • āt) *v.* To make others unfriendly to one; to remove or keep others at a distance; to estrange.
   *Politicians try hard not to **alienate** any voters.*

3. **anarchy** (an′ ar • kē) *n.* Disorder; no rule; the absence of government; chaos.
   *In the Wild West, years ago, **anarchy** existed because there were no laws.*

4. **autocracy** (aw • tok′ ruh • sē) *n.* A form of government in which one person possesses unlimited power.
   *In any **autocracy**, the head of government has absolute control of the country.*

5. **creditor** (kred′ ut • ur) *n.* One to whom a sum of money or other thing is due.
   *Savings and loan associations are more likely to be large **creditors** to the public through home purchase loans than are commercial banks.*

6. **demagogue** (dem′ uh • gog) *n.* A person who stirs up the emotions of people in order to become a leader and achieve selfish ends.
   ***Demagogues** are usually highly persuasive speakers who play on the emotions of the crowds for their own selfish ends.*

7. **emigrate** (em′ uh • grāt) *v.* To leave one's country or residence for elsewhere.
   *During the war, many immigrants **emigrated** to the United States.*

8. **monopoly** (muh • nop′ uh • lē) *n.* Excessive control of a commodity or service in a given market; control that makes possible the fixing of prices and the elimination of free competition.
   *If you have a **monopoly** in a certain market, you can then charge whatever you feel you can get away with charging.*

9. **monotonous** (muh • not′ uh • nus) *adj.* Uniform; dull; changeless; having no variety.

   *It is **monotonous** to do the same job over and over again.*

10. **speculate** (spek′ yuh • lāt) *v.* To take part in any risky business venture; to think about something by going over it in your mind and viewing it in all its aspects and relations.

    *Because I only like sure things, I do not gamble or **speculate** in the stock market.*

MUTTS

©Patrick McDonnell. Reprinted with special permission of King Features Syndicate.

Practices

PRACTICE A

Directions: Choose a word from the word list that *best* fits the blank in each sentence.

WORD LIST

alias	alienate	anarchy	autocracy	creditor
demagogue	emigrate	monopoly	monotonous	speculate

1. Several undocumented or illegal aliens said they would _____ to a country where they could make a living.

2. A(n) _____ often uses her powers of persuasion to make the people feel that she is interested in them, even though she isn't.

3. After the violent hurricane, many store windows were broken, and there seemed to be _____ throughout the city when people started looting the stores.

4. The criminal used a(n) _____ instead of his real name.

5. Please tell Marisa to give me another job because it is _____ to have to do the same thing over and over.

6. That company is trying to get a(n) _____ over the computer market so it can control the price of computers.

7. I would rather be a(n) _____ than a borrower.

8. Jason likes to _____ on new ventures, so if you need investors for your new business venture, contact him.

9. In a(n) _____, the ruler has absolute power.

10. In the film, the protagonists seemed to _____ themselves from their parents by doing everything possible to make them angry.

> **STOP.** *Check answers at the back of the book on page 251.*

PRACTICE B

Directions: Define the following words.

1. Alias _____

2. Alienate _____

3. Anarchy _____

4. Autocracy _____

5. Creditor _____

6. Demagogue _____

7. Emigrate _____

8. Monopoly _____

9. Monotonous _____

10. Speculate _____

> **STOP.** *Check answers at the end of the book on page 251.*

PRACTICE C

Directions: Match the word in Column A to its meaning in Column B.

	Column A	*Column B*
_____	1. alias	a. disorder
_____	2. alienate	b. to make others unfriendly to one
_____	3. anarchy	c. to take part in a risky venture
_____	4. autocracy	d. excessive control of a commodity
_____	5. creditor	e. government with one person having unlimited power
_____	6. demagogue	f. another name
_____	7. emigrate	g. a person who uses others for selfish ends
_____	8. monopoly	h. one to whom money is owed
_____	9. monotonous	i. dull
_____	10. speculate	j. to leave one's country for elsewhere

LESSON 48

anonymous	antipathy	centipede	claustrophobia	credential
creed	emancipate	nadir	symbiotic	unilateral

1. **anonymous** (uh • non′ uh • mus) *adj.* Lacking a name; of unknown authorship.
   *Most newspapers will not publish **anonymous** letters.*

2. **antipathy** (an • tip′ uh • thē) *n.* A dislike for someone.
   *Maria had great **antipathy** toward those who had hurt her brother.*

3. **centipede** (sent′ uh • pēd) *n.* Wormlike animal with many legs.
   *The **centipede** crawled along on its many feet.*

4. **claustrophobia** (klaus • truh • fō′ bē • uh) *n.* An extreme fear of being confined in a small place or a room.
   *It's horrible to be stuck in a small area such as an elevator when you suffer from **claustrophobia**.*

5. **credential** (kruh • den′ shul) *n.* A document such as a degree, diploma, or certificate; something that promises one to credit or confidence; something that makes others believe in a person.
   *Doctors need certain **credentials** to practice medicine.*

6. **creed** (krēd) *n.* A statement of religious belief; belief; principles.
   *The **creed** "All men are created equal" is found in our Constitution.*

7. **emancipate** (ē • man′ suh • pāt) *v.* To set free; to free; to release from bondage or servitude.
   *President Lincoln **emancipated** the slaves in all territories still at war with the Union in his Emancipation Proclamation, which became effective January 1, 1863.*

8. **nadir** (nā′ dur) *n.* The lowest point; opposite to the zenith, which is the highest point.
   *When a person is at his **nadir**, he is at a very low point in his life.*

9. symbiotic (sim • bē′ ot • ik) *adj.* Referring to the intimate relationship of two organisms living together, usually in a mutually advantageous situation; referring to mutual interdependence.

*Many instructors claim that research and teaching are a **symbiotic** relationship for them.*

10. unilateral (ū • nuh • lat′ er • ul) *adj.* Occurring on one side only; one-sided; done by one only.

*In many democratic organizations, the decisions by management are usually made by a group of people rather than in a **unilateral** way by individual executives.*

Practices

PRACTICE A

Directions: Match the meaning with the word from the word list.

WORD LIST

anonymous	antipathy	centipede	claustrophobia	credential
creed	emancipate	nadir	symbiotic	unilateral

1. Do you have any special _____ by which you live?

2. José said that he felt as though he was at the _____ rather than zenith of his existence.

3. When the wormlike _____ crawled toward me, I admit that I screamed.

4. I am not in servitude, but I feel as though I am when it comes to practicing the piano, so I am grateful for Karin for find ways to _____ me from practicing.

5. If you have _____, it is horrible to be stuck in a small elevator.

6. When I graduated from college, I received my diploma, an important _____.

7. The author said that he wanted to remain _____, so we didn't tell anyone his name.

8. We were dismayed when the decision was a(n) _____ one rather than one in which we were all involved.

9. A(n) _____ relationship is necessary when two things are interdependent.

10. My parents taught us not to have bad feelings or _____ toward others.

> **STOP.** *Check answers at the back of the book on page 251.*

PRACTICE B

Directions: Define the following words.

1. Anonymous _____

2. Antipathy _____

3. Centipede _____

4. Claustrophobia _____

-5. Credential _____

6. Creed _____

7. Emancipate _____

8. Nadir _____

9. Symbiotic _____

10. Unilateral _____

> **STOP.** *Check answers at the back of the book on page 251.*

PRACTICE C

Directions: Match the number of the word in Column A to the letter of its meaning in Column B.

Column A	*Column B*
_____ 1. anonymous	a. dislike
_____ 2. antipathy	b. lacking a name
_____ 3. centipede	c. the lowest point
_____ 4. claustrophobia	d. one-sided
_____ 5. credential	e. belief
_____ 6. creed	f. wormlike animal with many legs

_____ 7. emancipate   g. mutual interdependence

_____ 8. nadir   h. to free

_____ 9. symbiotic   i. extreme fear of being confined

_____ 10. unilateral   j. something that makes others believe
                                in a person

Multiple-Choice Assessment of Lessons 46–48

Directions: Words are arranged by lesson. Underline the meaning that *best* fits the word. Answers are at the back of the book. **If you miss any word meaning, go back to the lesson and restudy the word.**

LESSON 46

1. accreditation
  a. power
  b. college
  c. a vouching for
  d. earn a diploma

2. disparity
  a. unsure
  b. unlikeness
  c. refers to distance
  d. refers to two

3. endemic
  a. refers to end
  b. refers to natives
  c. bad
  d. native to an area

4. exacerbate
  a. to irritate
  b. to boost
  c. to boast
  d. to become hot

5. microbe
  a. a microorganism
  b. refers to dirt
  c. a gene
  d. disease

6. phobia
  a. refers to elevators
  b. a lens
  c. fear
  d. extreme

7. purify
  a. to make sure
  b. to make dirty
  c. to help
  d. to purge

8. putrid
  a. smelter
  b. causing unhappiness
  c. foul-smelling
  d. causing fear

9. succinct
  a. a point
  b. refers to a sink
  c. refers to sucking
  d. concise

10. unison
  a. agreement
  b. refers to a union
  c. harmonious agreement
  d. refers to harmonious

LESSON 47

11. alias
   a. another person
   b. another child
   c. another
   d. another name

12. alienate
   a. from another country
   b. to be a friend
   c. distance
   d. to make others unfriendly to one

13. anarchy
   a. chaos
   b. order
   c. to put in order
   d. refers to rule

14. autocracy
   a. refers to a ruler
   b. government
   c. refers to rule
   d. ruler with unlimited power in a government

15. creditor
   a. a debt
   b. refers to savings
   c. refers to a person
   d. one to whom money is owed

16. demagogue
   a. a leader
   b. refers to emotions
   c. a selfish leader
   d. refers to a god

17. emigrate
   a. wander
   b. someone who is an illegal alien
   c. to leave one's country for elsewhere
   d. to move from one's country to elsewhere

18. monopoly
   a. refers to control
   b. controls a commodity
   c. eliminates prices
   d. refers to competition

19. monotonous
   a. refers to a change
   b. refers to uniforms
   c. dull
   d. changing clothes

20. speculate
   a. risky business
   b. to involve oneself in risky business
   c. a venture
   d. refers to business

LESSON 48

21. anonymous
   a. lacking
   b. refers to a name
   c. lacking a name
   d. refers to unknown

22. antipathy
   a. refers to likes
   b. refers to dislikes
   c. a dislike of someone
   d. poor taste

23. centipede
   a. a worm
   b. wormlike animal
   c. refers to many legs
   d. wormlike animal with many legs

24. claustrophobia
   a. refers to fear
   b. fear of land
   c. a fear of heights
   d. fear of closed-in places

25. credential
   a. refers to credit
   b. a document
   c. a believer
   d. document such as a diploma

26. creed
   a. a believer
   b. a statement
   c. belief
   d. refers to religion

27. emancipate
   a. freedom
   b. refers to servitude
   c. to free
   d. refers to the Civil War

28. nadir
   a. highest point
   b. refers to opposite
   c. lowest point
   d. the zenith

29. symbiotic
   a. interdependence
   b. mutual interdependence
   c. two organisms
   d. refers to living together

30. unilateral
   a. refers to sides
   b. one-sided
   c. refers to decisions
   d. management decisions

STOP. *Check answers at the back of the book on page 251.*

LESSON 49

WORDS

anthropomorphic	genealogy	misogamist	omnipotent	omnipresent
omniscient	polygamy	potential	pungent	vicissitude

1. **anthropomorphic** (an • thruh • pō • mor′ fik) *adj.* Giving human shape or characteristics to gods, objects, animals, and so on.
   *Have you noticed how many **anthropomorphic** characteristics the animals have in Walt Disney films?*

2. **genealogy** (jē • nē • al′ uh • jē) *n.* The science or study of one's descent; a tracing of one's ancestors.
   *It is hard to trace the **genealogy** of your family if you do not know anything about your ancestors.*

3. **misogamist** (mi • sog′ uh • mist) *n.* Hater of marriage.
   *You cannot assume that someone is a **misogamist** because he is not married.*

4. **omnipotent** (om • nip′ uh • tent) *adj.* All-powerful.
   *The protagonist on the show was presented as being **omnipotent**, that is, as someone who was all-powerful.*

5. **omnipresent** (om • nē • prez′ unt) *adj.* Being present everywhere at all times.
   *It's hard to avoid some **omnipresent** television commercials; every time I turn on the TV, they seem to be showing.*

6. **omniscient** (om • nish′ ent) *adj.* All-knowing.
   *With the rapid increase of knowledge, it is not possible for someone to be **omniscient**, that is, all-knowing.*

7. **polygamy** (puh • lig′ uh • mē) *n.* Marriage to many spouses at the same time.
   *In some Middle Eastern nations, where **polygamy** is allowed, some very wealthy men are married to many wives at the same time.*

8. potential (puh • ten' shul) *n.* The possible ability one has. *adj.* Having force or power to develop.

*The acorn has the **potential** to become a huge oak tree.*

9. pungent (pun' junt) *adj.* Producing a sharp sensation of taste and smell; acrid; poignant; painful; sharp and piercing to the mind; biting; expressive; keenly clever, stimulating.

*The relish on my hot dog was so **pungent** that it literally made my eyes water.*

10. vicissitude (vuh • sis' uh • tūd) *n.* A condition of constant change; difficulty that is likely to occur or that is inherent in a situation. (pl.) Unpredictable changes or variations that occur in life, fortune, or otherwise.

*When Latisha didn't make the soccer team, her mother said that it was the **vicissitude** of life that she tried out for the team the same year as so many players better than she.*

Practices

PRACTICE A

Directions: Choose a word from the word list that *best* fits the blank in each sentence.

WORD LIST

anthropomorphic	genealogy	misogamist	omnipotent	omnipresent
omniscient	polygamy	potential	pungent	vicissitude

1. The _____ of the situation made me think twice before I decided to proceed because things could change unexpectedly.

2. Many of the Disney films have animals with _____ characteristics.

3. Carman said that Peter had the _____ to do the work, but he just refused to buckle down to do it.

4. Arthur said that he was not a(n) _____, it's just that he didn't want to get married yet.

5. & 6. No humans are both _____, that is, all powerful, and _____, that is, all knowing.

7. Ben said that he was having a difficult time tracing his _____ because he was adopted and didn't know who his biological parents were.

8. Even though it is against the law to practice _____ in the United States, some people have been known to do so.

9. Every time I put on the TV, I see a(n) _____ commercial urging people to go to a computer school.

10. His _____ words really surprised us because we had never heard him use such biting language before.

> **STOP.** *Check answers at the back of the book on page 251.*

PRACTICE B

Directions: Define the following words.

1. Anthropomorphic _____

2. Genealogy _____

3. Misogamist _____

4. Omnipotent _____

5. Omnipresent _____

6. Omniscient _____

7. Polygamy _____

8. Potential _____

9. Pungent _____

10. Vicissitude _____

> **STOP.** *Check answers at the back of the book on page 251.*

PRACTICE C

Directions: Match the number of the word in Column A to the letter of its meaning in Column B.

Column A

_____ 1. anthropomorphic

_____ 2. genealogy

_____ 3. misogamist

_____ 4. omnipotent

_____ 5. omnipresent

_____ 6. omniscient

_____ 7. polygamy

_____ 8. potential

_____ 9. pungent

_____ 10. vicissitude

Column B

a. being present everywhere at all times

b. all-powerful

c. all-knowing

d. marriage to many spouses at one time

e. giving human characteristics to animals

f. tracing of one's ancestors

g. condition of constant change

h. hater of marriage

i. possible ability one has

j. acrid

LESSON 50

capitulate	chronological	collateral	convocation	misnomer
perception	pseudonym	specious	synthesis	trauma

1. **capitulate** (kuh • pich′ uh • lāt) *v.* To give up (to an enemy) on prearranged conditions; to surrender; to yield.
   *The warriors said they would **capitulate** if they were granted certain rights.*

2. **chronological** (kron • uh • loj′ uh • kul) *adj.* Arranged in time order whereby earlier things or events precede later ones.
   *If you want to arrange events in **chronological** order, you need to know their dates.*

3. **collateral** (kuh • lat′ ur • ul) *adj.* Adjacent; side by side; parallel in time, rank, importance, and so on. *n.* Stocks or bonds or any property given as security for a mortgage to protect the lender.
   *When Beth and her husband took out a home mortgage, they pledged the property as **collateral**.*

4. **convocation** (con • vuh • kā′ shun) *n.* The act of calling together people for a meeting; an academic or church assembly.
   *At college, the professors were required to attend the academic **convocation**.*

5. **misnomer** (mis • nō′ mur) *n.* A name wrongly applied to something or someone; an error in the naming of a person or place in a legal document.
   *It is a **misnomer** to call a spider an insect because it is an arachnid with eight legs rather than six.*

6. **perception** (pur • sep′ shun) *n.* The act of becoming aware of something through the senses of seeing, hearing, smelling, feeling, and tasting.
   *If you have something wrong with your senses, your **perception** will be faulty.*

7. **pseudonym** (sū′ duh • nim) *n*. False name, especially used by an author to conceal his or her identity; a pen name.

*Samuel Clemens wrote under the name Mark Twain, his **pseudonym**.*

8. **specious** (spē′ shus) *adj*. Faulty reasoning.

*Though it seemed logical on the surface, on closer examination, Evan's argument provide to be **specious**, so we did not follow his advice.*

9. **synthesis** (sin′ thuh • sis) *n*. A putting together of two or more things to form a whole.

*We told the architect that we wanted a house that was a **synthesis** of all of our ideas.*

10. **trauma** (tra′ muh) *n*. A painful emotional experience often producing a lasting psychic effect; a bodily injury, wound, or shock.

*When John's psychology professor asked the students if any of them had ever experienced a **trauma**, John said it seemed as though his whole life was made up of ordeals.*

Practices

PRACTICE A

Directions: Choose a word from the word list that *best* fits the blank in each sentence.

WORD LIST

capitulate	chronological	collateral	convocation	misnomer
perception	pseudonym	specious	synthesis	trauma

1. My doctor said that I had suffered a(n) _____ to my body when I was hit by the car.

2. During World War II, the Japanese did not _____ until after the atom bomb was dropped on two cities in their country.

3. David's argument seemed logical to those unfamiliar with the information, but our instructor proved it to be _____.

4. Conan Doyle used a(n) _____ when he signed his books.

5. Our history instructor said to make sure that our dates were in _____ order.

6. We put our house up as _____ when we went to the bank for a loan.

7. What is your _____ of José's brother?

8. Is it a(n) _____ to call Kelsey by a different name?

9. Our school has a special _____ at the beginning and end of the school year.

10. Analysis and _____, which has to do with the putting together of something, are important skills that a person needs to be a good thinker.

> **STOP.** *Check answers at the back of the book on page 251.*

PRACTICE B

Directions: Define the following words.

1. Capitulate _____

2. Chronological _____

3. Collateral _____

4. Convocation _____

5. Misnomer _____

6. Perception _____

7. Pseudonym _____

8. Specious_____

9. Synthesis _____

10. Trauma _____

> **STOP.** *Check answers at the back of the book on page 252.*

PRACTICE C

Directions: Match the number of the word in Column A with the letter of its meaning in Column B.

	Column A	Column B
_____	1. capitulate	a. arranged in time order
_____	2. chronological	b. adjacent

_____ 3. collateral	c. to surrender
_____ 4. convocation	d. painful emotional experience often producing a lasting effect
_____ 5. misnomer	e. academic assembly
_____ 6. perception	f. false name
_____ 7. pseudonym	g. a putting together
_____ 8. specious	h. faulty reasoning
_____ 9. synthesis	i. a name wrongly applied
_____ 10. trauma	j. becoming aware of something through the senses

WORDS

dialect	extemporaneous	facsimile	faction	infinitesimal
manipulation	putative		travesty	ubiquitous	vestige

1. **dialect** (dī′ uh • lekt) *n.* A variety of speech; a regional form of standard English.
   *It's obvious to most people that Melissa comes from the South because she speaks with a southern **dialect**.*

2. **extemporaneous** (ek • stem • puh • rā′ nē • us) *adj.* Spoken without any preparation; spoken with some preparation but not written out or memorized beforehand; improvised.
   *Amid is very adept at giving **extemporaneous** speeches.*

3. **facsimile** (fak • sim′ uh • lē) *n.* An exact copy. *v.* To make an exact copy of; the transmission of graphic material by electronic means.
   *The police sent a **facsimile** of the mugger's face to the other police stations in town over the wire.*

4. **faction** (fak′ shun) *n.* A number of people in an organization, group, government, party, and so forth having a common goal, often self-seeking and reckless of the common good.
   *There was a special **faction** at our school that was trying to get control of the whole student body.*

5. **infinitesimal** (in • fin • uh • tes′ uh • mul) *adj.* Too small to be measured; very minute.
   *Because the microbe was **infinitesimal** in size, it could only be seen with the most high-powered microscope.*

6. **manipulation** (muh • nip′ yuh • lā • shun) *n.* The act of handling or operating; the act of managing or controlling skillfully or by shrewd use of influence; the act of changing or falsifying for one's own purpose or profit.
   *By the clever **manipulation** of all those around him, he was able to gain the position he desired.*

7. **putative** (pū′ tuh • tiv) *adj.* Commonly accepted or supposed; assumed to exist or to have existed.
   *The novelist kept referring to a **putative** ancestor of the protagonist.*

8. **travesty** (trav′ is • tē) *n.* A crude, distorted, or ridiculous imitation for purposes of ridicule; a burlesque.
   *There have been some trials that many people refer to as a **travesty** of justice.*

9. **ubiquitous** (ū • bik′ wuh • tus) *adj.* Present or seeming to be present everywhere at the same time; omnipresent.
   *The **ubiquitous** commercial seemed to be on all television channels at once.*

10. **vestige** (ves′ tij) *n.* A trace, mark, or sign of something that once existed but doesn't anymore.
    *There was no **vestige** of any trees, yet the area used to be covered by them.*

Practices

PRACTICE A

Directions: Choose a word from the word list that *best* fits the blank in each sentence.

WORD LIST

dialect	extemporaneous	facsimile	faction	infinitesimal
manipulation	putative	travesty	ubiquitous	vestige

1. We could find no _____ of him anywhere.

2. Have you noticed how people who come from New England states often speak with a certain _____?

3. Our speech instructor said that we would each have to present a(n) _____ speech on a topic of our choice.

4. Isn't Ahmid an almost exact _____ of his father when he was Ahmid's age?

5. That _____ had very strong backing from various politicians in our district.

6. Have you noticed that some advertisements are _____?

7. When my instructor speaks, he seems to make a(n) _____ of the English language.

8. My mother always speaks of one of my _____ ancestors.

9. I feel that bug is _____ because I cannot see it.

10. My boss is always trying to do something that involves the _____ of others.

> **STOP.** *Check answers at the back of the book on page 252.*

PRACTICE B

Directions: Define the following words.

1. Dialect _____

2. Extemporaneous _____

3. Facsimile _____

4. Faction _____

5. Infinitesimal _____

6. Manipulation _____

7. Putative _____

8. Travesty _____

9. Ubiquitous _____

10. Vestige _____

> **STOP.** *Check answers at the back of the book on page 252.*

PRACTICE C

Directions: Match the number of the word in Column A to the letter of its meaning in Column B.

	Column A		Column B
_____	1. dialect	a.	number of persons in an organization
_____	2. extemporaneous	b.	too small to be measured
_____	3. facsimile	c.	crude imitation for ridicule purposes
_____	4. faction	d.	omnipresent
_____	5. infinitesimal	e.	commonly accepted
_____	6. manipulation	f.	exact copy
_____	7. putative	g.	spoken without preparation
_____	8. travesty	h.	trace of something that once existed
_____	9. ubiquitous	i.	a variety of speech
_____	10. vestige	j.	act of handling

Multiple-Choice Assessment of Lessons 49–51

Directions: Words are arranged by lesson. Underline the meaning that *best* fits the word. Answers are at the back of the book. **If you miss any word meaning, go back to the lesson and restudy the word.**

LESSON 49

1. anthropomorphic
  a. refers to humans
  b. giving human characteristics to animals
  c. forms
  d. helping animals

2. genealogy
  a. refers to genes
  b. a science
  c. tracing one's ancestors
  d. the science of genes

3. misogamist
 a. hater of marriage
 b. refers to hate
 c. refers to marriage
 d. an unmarried person

4. omnipotent
 a. powerful person
 b. refers to power
 c. refers to all
 d. all-powerful

5. omnipresent
 a. all-powerful
 b. being present everywhere
 c. refers to being present
 d. refers to all times

6. omniscient
 a. refers to all
 b. all-powerful
 c. all-knowing
 d. present everywhere

7. polygamy
 a. married
 b. married to many at the same
  time
 c. married to many people
 d. a type of marriage

8. potential
 a. refers to power
 b. a power machine
 c. possible ability
 d. energy in motion

9. pungent
 a. refers to smell
 b. acrid
 c. refers to ability
 d. piercing noise

10. vicissitude
 a. refers to something constant
 b. refers to life
 c. refers to vice
 d. constant change

LESSON 50

11. capitulate
 a. surrender
 b. being taken prisoner
 c. refers to capture
 d. helpless

12. chronological
 a. time
 b. arranged in time order
 c. refers to arrangements
 d. refers to clocks

13. collateral
 a. necessary for mortgages
 b. security
 c. something given
 d. security given to protect

14. convocation
 a. an assembly
 b. calling people
 c. an academic assembly
 d. calling people together

15. misnomer
 a. a name
 b. a wrongly applied name
 c. calling someone names
 d. refers to names

16. perception
 a. refers to senses
 b. aware through the senses
 c. being aware
 d. the sense of smell

17. **pseudonym**
    a. alias
    b. refers to false
    c. refers to name
    d. refers to fear

18. **specious**
    a. reasoning
    b. faulty reasoning
    c. faulty
    d. special

19. **synthesis**
    a. putting together
    b. important for thinking
    c. a breaking down
    d. refers to whole

20. **trauma**
    a. refers to pain
    b. refers to memory
    c. a bodily injury
    d. refers to psychology

LESSON 51

21. **dialect**
    a. refers to speech
    b. not proper speech
    c. variety of speech
    d. hateful speech

22. **extemporaneous**
    a. done in school
    b. prepared speech
    c. unprepared speech
    d. quick speech

23. **facsimile**
    a. same child
    b. exact copy
    c. refers to copy
    d. a wrong image

24. **faction**
    a. numbers of people
    b. a group
    c. different people
    d. people having same goal

25. **infinitesimal**
    a. very minute
    b. ending
    c. never ending
    d. refers to measurement

26. **manipulation**
    a. refers to man
    b. managing shrewdly
    c. refers to managing
    d. refers to falsification

27. **putative**
    a. refers to a put down
    b. refers to putting into action
    c. commonly accepted
    d. refers to ancestors

28. **travesty**
    a. journey
    b. a traveler
    c. travels
    d. crude imitation to ridicule

29. **ubiquitous**
    a. omnipresent
    b. refers to present
    c. everywhere
    d. at the same time

30. **vestige**
    a. a vessel
    b. refers to tracing
    c. a trace
    d. refers to signs

STOP. *Check answers at the back of the book on page 252.*

LESSON 52

1. **browser** (browz′ ur) *n.* Software that allows a user to search through information on a server.
   *Lisa used her **browser** to search for information about phonics.*

2. **cineplex** (sin′ uh • pleks) *n.* A cinema complex; a building with several movie theaters.
   *When we went to the local **cineplex**, we couldn't decide on the movie we wanted to see because there were so many choices.*

3. **cloning** (klōn′ ing) *n.* The technique of producing a genetically identical duplicate of an organism by replacing the nucleus of an unfertilized ovum with a nucleus of a body cell from the organism.
   *There is a lot of controversy concerning **cloning** because some people fear that scientists may try to produce cloned children.*

4. **cybernetics** (sī • bur • net′ iks) *n.* The science dealing with the study of human control systems such as the brain and nervous systems and complex electronic systems.
   *The twenty-first century will probably be known eventually as the age of **cybernetics** because of all the work being done in this area.*

5. **cyberspace** (sī′ bur • spās) *n.* The electronic system of interlinked networks of computers that is a boundless environment that provides access to all kinds of information and interactive communication.
   *Many people go to **cyberspace** to get information on various topics and even to find soulmates.*

6. **e-mail**—short for electronic mail (ē′ māl) *n.* Messages distributed by electronic means, especially from one computer system to one or more recipients. *v.* The act of sending such a message.

*Now that students can send **e-mail** to their teachers when they miss a class, they have no excuse for not knowing assignments.*

7. **hacker** (hak′ ur) *n.* A person very adept at computer programming and working with computers; a talented amateur user of computers; one who attempts to gain illegal access to files in various systems.

*The computer age has given rise to **hackers,** a new kind of criminal who can use their skills to break into secured systems.*

8. **interactive** (in • tur • ak′ tiv) *adj.* Acting on one another; programming electronic equipment that allows people to participate; a mode of operation in which there is a continual exchange of information between the computer and the person at a viewer screen.

*Almost every piece of electronic equipment that I presently buy says that it allows for **interactive** communication.*

9. **Internet** (in′ tur • net) *n.* An extensive computer network made up of thousands of other business, academic, and governmental networks.

*Most people today seem to have computers that are hooked up to the **Internet**.*

10. **scanner** (skan′ ur) *n.* An electronic or optical device that senses or records information for modification, storage, or transmission.

*I am pleased that my college department recently bought a **scanner** because now I can scan in my children's pictures in my greeting cards.*

Practices

PRACTICE A

Directions: Choose the word from the word list that *best* fits in the blank. A word may be used once only. If necessary, you may also change the form of the word in the word list.

WORD LIST

browser	cineplex	cloning	cybernetics	cyberspace
e-mail	hacker	interactive	Internet	scanner

Our friend Anna is known to everyone as a computer expert. But she is a(n)

(1) _____ who has entered people's computers illegally. We keep

telling her that she better be careful because she is going to wind up in prison. She just shrugs us off. "This is the age of (2)_____ reality. It's the age of being there, of participating." We agree, but we do not like what she is doing. We all use (3)_____ to help us search for needed information on a server on the (4)_____. We also use a (5)_____ to record some information we want loaded into our computers, but we never resort to anything that is illegal. One day, we went to the local (6)_____; it was hard to decide on a film because there were so many movies available, but we decided to see a film on (7)_____.The idea of duplicating an identical person from just a cell intrigued us. While we were waiting for the movie to start, Anna said she had decided to major in (8)_____, which deals with complex electronic systems. She said that she had (9)_____ her vita to a well-known person in the field and he had recommended that because she did so much work in the area of (10)_____, the science she had homed in on seemed right for her.

> **STOP.** *Check answers at the back of the book on page 252.*

PRACTICE B

Directions: Define the following words.

1. Browser _____

2. Cineplex _____

3. Cloning _____

4. Cybernetics _____

5. Cyberspace _____

6. E-mail _____

7. Hacker _____

8. Interactive _____

9. Internet _____

10. Scanner _____

STOP. *Check answers at the back of the book on page 252.*

PRACTICE C

Directions: Match the number of the word in Column A with the letter of its meaning in Column B.

	Column A	*Column B*
_____	1. browser	a. acting on one another
_____	2. cineplex	b. person adept with computers
_____	3. cloning	c. electronic mail
_____	4. cybernetics	d. optical device that records information
_____	5. cyberspace	e. extensive computer network
_____	6. e-mail	f. producing genetically identical duplicates
_____	7. hacker	g. electronic system of interlinked computer networks
_____	8. interactive	h. science dealing with human control systems
_____	9. Internet	i. a cinema complex
_____	10. scanner	j. software that allows users to search information on a server

Answers

LESSON 1

Practice A. 1. stagnant, 2. modify, 3. frugal, 4. liability, 5. conservative, 6. liberal, 7. covet, 8. asset, 9. economize, 10. allot

Practice B. 1. spend wisely, 2. broadminded; traditional, 3. thrifty, 4. advantage; disadvantage, 5. distributes, 6.desires, 7. foul, 8. changes

LESSON 2

Practice A. 1. colleagues, 2. precedents, 3. reliable, 4. persevere, 5. interrogated, 6. reluctant, 7. significant, 8. intricate, 9. antecedent, 10. adaptation

Practice B. 1. example, 2. prior, 3. dependable, 4. unwilling, 5. important, 6. fellow members of a profession, 7. question, 8. complex, 9. modification, 10. persist

LESSON 3

Practice A. 1. coincidence, 2. dilemma, 3. pertinent, 4. affirm, 5. haughty, 6. isolate, 7. delete or eradicate, 8. delete or eradicate 9. disdain, 10. diligent

Practice B. 1. haughty, 2. destroy completely, 3. coincidence, 4. isolate, 5. affirm, 6. delete, 7. pertinent, 8. disdain, 9. diligent, 10. dilemma

MULTIPLE-CHOICE ASSESSMENT LESSONS 1–3

Lesson 1: (1) d, (2) c, (3) d, (4) c, (5) d, (6) d, (7) c, (8) b, (9) a, (10) a

Lesson 2: (11) d, (12) c, (13) d, (14) c, (15) a, (16) b, (17) a, (18) b, (19) c, (20) d

Lesson 3: (21) d, (22) c, (23) b, (24) d, (25) c, (26) c, (27) c, (28) b, (29) c, (30) c

LESSON 4

Practice A. 1. isolate, 2. naïve, 3. candid, 4. inquisitive, 5. frustrate, 6. tacit, 7. terse, 8. verbose, 9. integrate, 10. sustain

Practice B. 1. sustain, 2. naïve, 3. frustrate, 4. inquisitive, 5. candid, 6. tacit, 7. verbose, 8. integrate, 9. terse, 10. isolate

LESSON 5

Practice A. 1. alternative, 2. affluent, 3. optimist, 4. fatigued, 5. pessimist, 6. famished, 7. nostalgic, 8. mundane, 9. formidable, 10. concise

Practice B. 1. nostalgic, 2. fatigued, 3. formidable, 4. famished, 5. optimist, 6. pessimist, 7. mundane, 8. alternative, 9. terse, 10. affluent

LESSON 6

Practice A. 1. fictitious, 2. lethal, 3. fatal, 4. covert, 5. hostile, 6. relevant, 7. curtail, 8. amnesty, 9. overt, 10. sentimental

Practice B. 1. covert, 2. fatal or lethal, 3. amnesty, 4. overt, 5. curtail, 6. relevant, 7. hostile, 8. fictitious, 9. sentimental, 10. lethal or fatal.

MULTIPLE-CHOICE ASSESSMENT LESSONS 4–6

Lesson 4 (1) c, (2) a, (3) a, (4) b, (5) b, (6) d, (7) c, (8) b, (9) c, (10) b

Lesson 5: (11) c, (12) c, (13) d, (14) b, (15) b, (16) a, (17) c, (18) d, (19) d, (20) b
Lesson 6: (21) b, (22) c, (23) b, (24) d, (25) b, (26) c, (27) d, (28) a, (29) d, (30) b

LESSON 7

Practice A. euphemism, 2. aesthetic, 3. affront, 4. antagonize, 5. derogatory, 6. attitude, 7. characteristic 8. intimidate, 9. hypocrite, 10. inclination
Practice B. 1. d, 2. c, 3. f, 4. a, 5. j, 6. b, 7. e, 8. i, 9. g, 10. h.

LESSON 8

Practice A. 1. infamous, 2. docile, 3. apprehensive, 4. discreet, 5. bland, 6. initiate, 7. miscellaneous, 8. omission, 9. scrutinized, 10. unanimous
Practice B. 1. c, 2. g, 3. j, 4. i, 5. f, 6. e, 7. h, 8. d, 9. b, 10. a

LESSON 9

Practice A. 1. versatile, 2. adept, 3. anecdote, 4. subsequent, 5. contagious, 6. curt; paradox 7. adversary, 8. acquisition, 9. variable
Practice B. 1. f, 2. a, 3. g, 4. h, 5. i, 6. j, 7. d, 8. c, 9. b, 10. e

MULTIPLE-CHOICE ASSESSMENT LESSONS 7–9

Lesson 7: (1) b, (2) a, (3) b, (4) a, (5) b, (6) c, (7) d, (8) d, (9) c, (10) a
Lesson 8: (11) c, (12) b, (13) c, (14) d, (15) d, (16) c, (17) a, (18) d, (19) b, (20) a
Lesson 9: (21) d, (22) b, (23) b, (24) d, (25) b, (26) a, (27) c, (28) d, (29) a, (30) b

LESSON 10

Practice A. 1. domestic, 2. exotic, 3.oxymoron, 4. irate, 5. mimic, 6. trite, 7. turmoil, 8. passive, 9. appraise, 10. gregarious
Practice B. 1. b, 2. c, 3. a, 4. e, 5. f, 6. h, 7. i, 8. g, 9. j, 10. d

LESSON 11

Practice A. 1. wary, 2. compromise, 3.apprise, 4. traditional; conform, 5. tact, 6. emulate, 7. plaintiffs, 8. crass, 9. pretense
Practice B. 1. to inform or notify, 2. to settle by both sides making concessions, 3. to behave in a conventional way, 4. insensitive; dull; blatantly money grubbing, 5. to imitate or copy, 6. the complainant in a court of law, 7. a false claim; make believe, 8. skill in dealing with people, 9. conventional, 10. cautious; careful

LESSON 12

Practice A. 1. awry, 2. expend, 3. spouse, 4. extricate, 5. assurance, 6. infidelity, 7. remorse, 8. assumption, 9. inevitable, 10. gullible
Practice B. 1. certainty, 2. husbands or wives, 3. use up, 4. anguish, 5. free, 6. supposition, 7. unfaithfulness, 8. wrong, 9. sure to happen, 10. easily deceived

MULTIPLE-CHOICE ASSESSMENT LESSONS 10–12

Lesson 10: (1) d, (2) a, (3) a, (4) c, (5) b, (6) c, (7) a, (8) b, (9) d, (10) c
Lesson 11: (11) a, (12) d, (13) a, (14) b, (15) b, (16) d, (17) a, (18) c, (19) c, (20) a
Lesson 12: (21) d, (22) b, (23) c, (24) d, (25) a, (26) b, (27) a, (28) d, (29) c, (30) d

LESSON 13

Practice A. 1. motivate, 2. skeptical, 3. idealist, 4. duration, 5. astute, 6. tedious, 7. anticipate, 8. cope, 9. reality, 10. charisma

Practice B. 1. tedious, 2. cope, 3. anticipate, 4. charisma, 5. idealist, 6. astute, 7. duration, 8. skeptical, 9. reality, 10. motivate

LESSON 14

Practice A. 1. protagonist, 2. subjective, 3. concept, 4. citation, 5. synopsis, 6. comprehensive, 7. paraphrase, 8. plagiarism, 9. cognitive, 10. objective

Practice B. 1. cognitive, 2. comprehensive, 3. subjective 4. objective, 5. protagonist, 6. synopsis, 7. concept, 8. citations, 9. plagiarism, 10. paraphrase

LESSON 15

Practice A. 1. exceedingly, 2. harmony, 3. discord, 4. durable, 5. literally, 6. prestige, 7. status, 8. dominant, 9. compatible, 10. dogmatic

Practice B. 1. dogmatic, 2. discord, 3. harmony, 4. exceedingly, 5. literally, 6. compatible, 7. status, 8. prestige, 9. dominant, 10. durable

MULTIPLE-CHOICE ASSSESSMENT LESSONS 13–15

Lesson 13: (1) c, (2) b, (3) d, (4) b, (5) d, (6) b, (7) d, (8) b, (9) a, (10) c

Lesson 14: (11) b, (12) a, (13) c, (14) d, (15) b, (16) b, (17) c, (18) c, (19) a, (20) d

Lesson 15: (21) b, (22) d, (23) b, (24) b, (25) c, (26) b, (27) c, (28) d, (29) b, (30) c

LESSON 16

Practice A. 1. adamant, 2. fetid, 3. disarray, 4. amoral, 5. implore, 6. amiable, 7. extent, 8. demoralize, 9. emanate, 10. avail

Practice B. 1. implore, 2. fetid, 3. disarray, 4. adamant, 5. emanate, 6. avail, 7. amiable, 8. demoralize 9. extent, 10. amoral

LESSON 17

Practice A. 1. saturated, 2. rancid, 3. extant, 4. meticulous, 5. encounter, 6. malign, 7. eccentric, 8. animosity, 9. absolve, 10. epitome

Practice B. 1. saturated, 2. epitome, 3. rancid, 4. absolve, 5. extant, 6. animosity, 7. malign, 8. eccentric, 9. encounter, 10. meticulous.

LESSON 18

Practice A. 1. d, 2. j, 3. a, 4. i, 5. g, 6. b, 7. h, 8. f, 9. e, 10. c

Practice B. 1. capable of being hurt, 2. voters, 3. turn away, 4. an opinion not in agreement with accepted doctrine, 5. advocated, 6. evaluate, 7. decline, 8. wide-spreading, 9. sluggish, 10. poll

MULTIPLE-CHOICE ASSSESSMENT LESSONS 16–18

Lesson 16: (1) a, (2) c, (3) b, (4) b, (5) d, (6) c, (7) a, (8) c, (9) c, (10) b

Lesson 17: (11) b, (12) a, (13) b, (14) a, (15) c, (16) d, (17) c, (18) b, (19) a, (20) a

Lesson 18: (21) d, (22) c, (23) d, (24) d, (25) b, (26) b, (27) c, (28) d, (29) b, (30) a

LESSON 19

Practice A. 1. feign, 2. taciturn, 3. livid, 4. equanimity, 5. caustic, 6. beguile, 7. intrigue, 8. apathy, 9. empathy, 10. opponent

Practice B. 1. indifferent, 2. deceive, 3. cutting; stinging, 4. imagine putting oneself into the skin of another, 5. composure; balance, 6. pretend, 7. secret or underhanded scheme, 8. furious, 9. adversary, 10. untalkative

LESSON 20

Practice A. 1. g, 2. c, 3. d, 4. b, 5. a, 6. h, 7. j, 8. i, 9. e, 10. f

Practice B. 1. ecstasy, 2. tentative, 3. temerity, 4. tenet, 5. terminate, 6. tenure, 7. taciturn, 8. versatile, 9. listless, 10. peruse

LESSON 21

Practice A. 1. h, 2. d, 3. e, 4. g, 5. f, 6. i, 7. a, 8. j, 9. c, 10. b

Practice B. 1. foreigner, 2. original model, 3. haughty, 4. odd, 5. act of restricting, 6. to hasten, 7. to obscure, 8. to fill again, 9. well filled, 10. economically wise

MULTIPLE-CHOICE ASSSESSMENT LESSONS 19–21

Lesson 19: (1) c, (2) c, (3) c, (4) d, (5) a, (6) c, (7) d, (8) d, (9) b, (10) b

Lesson 20: (11) d, (12) a, (13) a, (14) c, (15) d, (16) a, (17) c, (18) b, (19) c, (20) c

Lesson 21: (21) c, (22) b, (23) b, (24) a, (25) b, (26) b, (27) c, (28) a, (29) c, (30) c

LESSON 22

Practice A. 1. sedate, 2. laudable, 3. prudent, 4. vindicate, 5. castigate, 6. vital, 7. satiate, 8. virile, 9. vindictive, 10. awe

Practice B. 1. g, 2. i, 3. e, 4. b, 5. h, 6. c, 7. d, 8. j, 9. f, 10. a

LESSON 23

Practice A. 1. signify, 2. valid, 3. jeopardy, 4. invincible, 5. corroborate, 6. temperate, 7. repent, 8. criterion, 9. exonerate, 10. data

Practice B. 1. to confirm, 2. a standard of judging, 3. information given, 4. to clear of a charge of guilt, 5. impossible to overcome, 6. danger, 7. to feel regret, 8. moderate, 9. to be a sign of, 10. sound

LESSON 24

Practice A. 1. parse, 2. amend, 3. abridge, 4. attrition, 5. infinite, 6. futile, 7. finite, 8. imminent, 9. apt, 10. phenomenon

Practice B. 1. shorten, 2. change, 3. appropriate, 4. a gradual wearing away, 5. having an end, 6. useless, 7. about to happen, 8. having no end, 9. to separate a sentence into its parts, 10. something extremely unusual

MULTIPLE-CHOICE ASSSESSMENT LESSONS 22–24

Lesson 22: (1) c, (2) d, (3) b, (4) d, (5) a, (6) c, (7) b, (8) a, (9) b, (10) c

Lesson 23: (11) c, (12) c, (13) b, (14) a, (15) c, (16) c, (17) c, (18) a, (19) a, (20) c

Lesson 24: (21) d, (22) c, (23) c, (24) b, (25) c, (26) a, (27) c, (28) d, (29) d, (30) a

LESSON 25

Practice A. 1. deprecate, 2. redundant, 3. query, 4. compensate, 5. esoteric, 6. austere, 7. delve, 8. celibacy, 9. improvise, 10. abstract

Practice B. 1. not concrete, 2. severe, 3. the state of being unmarried, 4.to make up for, 5. to search, 6. to belittle, 7. hard to understand, 8. to do on the spur of the moment, 9. a question, 10. unnecessary

LESSON 26

Practice A. 1. dire, 2. pragmatic, 3. extrinsic, 4. intrinsic, 5. ominous, 6. ornate, 7. placid 8. libel, 9. morality, 10. feasible

Practice B. 1. morality, 2. feasible, 3. libel, 4. ominous, 5. placid, 6. pragmatic, 7. ornate 8. extrinsic, 9. intrinsic, 10. dire

LESSON 27

Practice A. 1. ridicule, 2. deference, 3. didactic, 4. poignant, 5. hypothesis, 6. contemporary, 7. pretentious, 8. eclectic, 9. convene, 10. affinity

Practice B. 1. attraction to another, 2. respect, 3. possible solution to a problem, 4. arousing pity, 5. make fun of, 6. to assemble, 7. modern, 8. showy, 9. made up of numerous things, 10. referring to teaching

MULTIPLE-CHOICE ASSSESSMENT LESSONS 25–27

Lesson 25: (1) c, (2) b, (3) c, (4) c, (5) a, (6) a, (7) c, (8) b, (9) c, (10) d

Lesson 26: (11) a, (12) b, (13) c, (14) b, (15) b, (16) d, (17) a, (18) b, (19) b, (20) a

Lesson 27: (21) d, (22) b, (23) c, (24) d, (25) a, (26) c, (27) d, (28) b, (29) a, (30) c

LESSON 28

Practice A. 1. glib, 2. impediment, 3. intrepid, 4. latent, 5. waive, 6. propriety, 7. itinerant, 8. enervate, 9. empirical, 10. placate

Practice B. 1. based solely on observation and experimentation, 2. to weaken, 3. done in a smooth manner, 4. obstacle, 5. fearless, 6. a traveler, 7. lying hidden, 8. to pacify, 9. the quality of being proper, 10. give up a right or claim

LESSON 29

Practice A. 1. fiscal, 2. authentic, 3. inclusive, 4. equivalent, 5. intense, 6. measurement, 7. deduction, 8. exclusive, 9. assess, 10. accountability

Practice B. 1. responsibility, 2. real, 3. subtraction, 4. equal, 5. to evaluate, 6. refers to all, 7. being only one of a kind, 8. refers to finances, 9. the extent or capacity of something, 10. very strong

LESSON 30

Practice A. 1. psychology, 2. theology, 3. biology, 4. civics, 5. philosophy, 6. ecology, 7. geology 8. astronomy, 9. astrology, 10. anthropology

Practice B. 1. the study of humankind, 2. the reading of the stars, 3. the study of the stars, 4. the study of life, 5. that part of political science dealing with citizens' affairs

6. the study of the relationship between the environment and living organisms, 7. the study of the earth's physical history and makeup, 8. the study of human knowledge, 9. the study of the mind, 10. the study of religion

MULTIPLE-CHOICE ASSSESSMENT LESSONS 28–30

Lesson 28: (1) b, (2) a, (3) c, (4) b, (5) c, (6) b, (7) d, (8) c, (9) b, (10) c

Lesson 29: (11) d, (12) d, (13) a, (14) d, (15) b, (16) c, (17) a, (18) a, (19) c, (20) a

Lesson 30: (21) d, (22) c, (23) a, (24) d, (25) d, (26) d, (27) c, (28) b, (29) c, (30) b

LESSON 31

Practice A. 1. ambiguous, 2. posthumously, 3. novice, 4. provoke, 5. belligerent, 6. civil, 7. pacify, 8. civilian, 9. civilization, 10. politics

Practice B. 1. posthumously, 2. belligerent, 3. civil, 4. civilian, 5. provoke, 6. ambiguous, 7. novice, 8. politics, 9. pacify 10. civilization

LESSON 32

Practice A. 1. defer, 2. procrastinate, 3. dissent, 4. dormant, 5. diffident, 6. divulge, 7. morbidity, 8. mortality, 9. hypertension, 10. lucid

Practice B. 1. lucid, 2. divulge, 3. dormant, 4. procrastinates, 5. mortality, 6. morbidity, 7. hypertension, 8. diffident, 9. dissent, 10. defer

LESSON 33

Practice A. 1. one who claims uncertainty, 2. ancient, 3. one who does not believe in the existence of God, 4. marriage to two spouses at the same time, 5. one concerned with oneself primarily, 6. refers to all in a group, 7. a charge, 8. something newly introduced, 9. a hater of humankind, 10. marriage to one person at one time

Practice B. 1. bigamy, 2. egocentric, 3. monogamy, 4. atheist, 5. agnostic, 6. innovation, 7. archaic, 8. misanthrope, 9. generic, 10. indictment

MULTIPLE-CHOICE ASSSESSMENT LESSONS 31–33

Lesson 31: (1) a, (2) d, (3) b, (4) d, (5) c, (6) a, (7) c, (8) b, (9) c, (10) b

Lesson 32: (11) b, (12) c, (13) d, (14) a, (15) d, (16) c, (17) b, (18) a, (19) c, (20) b

Lesson 33: (21) c, (22) c, (23) c, (24) b, (25) c, (26) a, (27) d, (28) c, (29) b, (30) b

LESSON 34

Practice A. 1. something out of time order, 2. hobby, 3. the statistical study of human populations, 4. born with, 5. forgiving of insults, 6. one very large city, made up of a number of cities, 7. the decline of business activity, 8. holding to one's views, 9. freely expressing oneself in speech, 10. a person's job

Practice B. 1. vocation, 2. avocation, 3. magnanimous, 4. tenacious, 5. vocal, 6. innate, 7. demography, 8. megalopolis, 9. anachronism, 10. recession

LESSON 35

Practice A. 1. quick and easy of movement, 2. approval, 3. one hundred years, 4. in the metric system, a unit of measure equal to 1/100 meter, 5. 10 meters, 6. to destroy but not completely, 7. in the metric system, a unit of length equal to 1/10 meter, 8. 1,000 meters, 9. 1,000,000 bits, 10. Period of 1,000 years

Practice B. 1. megabit, 2. millennium, 3. centennial, 4. approbation, 5. agile, 6. kilometer, 7. decimate, 8. decameter, 9. decimeter, 10. centimeter

LESSON 36

Practice A. 1. able to use both hands equally well, 2. easing of strained relations, 3. confinement, 4. to use ambiguous language on purpose, 5. to state in detail, 6. a ranting and inflated speech or writing, 7. not able to be changed back, 8. future generations, 9. lying on the back with face upward, 10. loud speech

Practice B. 1. vociferous, 2. harangue, 3. detention, 4. equivocate, 5. supine, 6. ambidextrous, 7. irrevocable, 8. posterity, 9. détente, 10. expound

MULTIPLE-CHOICE ASSSESSMENT LESSONS 34–36

Lesson 34: (1) a, (2) c, (3) d, (4) b, (5) c, (6) d, (7) c, (8) a, (9) c, (10) a
Lesson 35: (11) a, (12) c, (13) d, (14) b, (15) d, (16) b, (17) d, (18) b, (19) a, (20) c
Lesson 36: (21) b, (22) c, (23) a, (24) c, (25) b, (26) b, (27) c, (28) b, (29) b, (30) c

LESSON 37

Practice A. 1. to make alive, 2. hatred, 3. to remove from a high position, 4. a saying, 5. one's usual frame of mind, 6. different, 7. belief, 8. secret, 9. mixed, 10. being uniform throughout

Practice B. 1. furtive, 2. heterogeneous, 3. animate, 4. diverse, 5. dogma, 6. dictum, 7. disposition, 8. animosity, 9. depose, 10. homogeneous

LESSON 38

Practice A. 1. warlike, 2. bad, 3. wandering, 4. relevant, 5. gross exaggeration, 6. stubborn, 7. governing by a father figure, 8. boundary line, 9. optimistic person, 10. a ghost responsible for mysterious noisy disturbances

Practice B. 1. Pollyanna, 2. bellicose, 3. periphery, 4. erratic, 5. egregious, 6. hyperbole, 7. obdurate, 8. poltergeist, 9. germane, 10. paternalism

LESSON 39

Practice A. 1. act of causing a painless death, 2. outrageous, 3. very important person, 4. treacherous, 5. acceptable, 6. person supposedly sensitive to forces beyond physical world, 7. person suffering from a mental disorder, 8. resistance or rebellion against government in power, 9. faulty reasoning, 10. a wage

Practice B. 1. sophistry, 2. flagrant, 3. psychic, 4. perfidious, 5. plausible, 6. psychopath, 7. euthanasia, 8. magnate, 9. stipend, 10. sedition

MULTIPLE-CHOICE ASSSESSMENT LESSONS 37–39

Lesson 37: (1) b, (2) d, (3) a, (4) c, (5) d, (6) a, (7) a, (8) d, (9) c, (10) c
Lesson 38: (11) c, (12) c, (13) b, (14) a, (15) c, (16) d, (17) b, (18) c, (19) b, (20) d
Lesson 39: (21) b, (22) a, (23) d, (24) c, (25) c, (26) d, (27) b, (28) c, (29) b, (30) a

LESSON 40

Practice A. 1. a lover of books, 2. books used as guidance, 3. to gather together in order, 4. to forgive, 5. harmonious, 6. vigor, 7. systematic killing of a whole group of people, 8. honesty, 9. word for word, 10. greedy in some desire

Practice B. 1. bibliophile, 2. verbatim, 3. condone, 4. euphonious, 5. collate, 6. veracity, 7. bibliotherapy, 8. voracious, 9. genocide, 10. euphoria

LESSON 41

Practice A. 1. general agreement, 2. tending to turn from what is normal in a group, 3. to deviate, 4. to destroy completely, 5. fawning, 6. a man who engages in insincere love affairs, 7. pure, 8. to lure, 9. ungrammatical use of words, 10. substitute

Practice B. 1. solecism, 2. seduce, 3. consensus, 4. obliterate, 5. pristine, 6. surrogate, 7. obsequious, 8. deviant, 9. diverge, 10. philanderer

LESSON 42

Practice A. 1. anxiety, 2. to absorb into one's thinking, 3. intense dislike, 4. division into two parts, 5. able to speak and write easily, 6. central, 7. period of level stability, 8. full, 9. knowledgeable person, 10. to give in

Practice B. 1. aversion, 2. pivotal, 3. plenary, 4. pundit, 5. relent, 6. fluent, 7. angst, 8. plateau, 9. dichotomy, 10. assimilate

MULTIPLE-CHOICE ASSSESSMENT LESSONS 40–42

Lesson 40: (1) b, (2) c, (3) d, (4) d, (5) c, (6) b, (7) b, (8) a, (9) c, (10) c

Lesson 41: (11) b, (12) c, (13) a, (14) a, (15) c, (16) d, (17) b, (18) d, (19) d, (20) c

Lesson 42: (21) b, (22) d, (23) a, (24) c, (25) d, (26) b, (27) b, (28) b, (29) b, (30) a

LESSON 43

Practice A. 1. epiphany, 2. adversity, 3. corpulent, 4. expediency, 5. graphic, 6. abyss, 7. discourse, 8. introvert, 9. subtle, 10. fortify

Practice B. 1. a bottomless gulf, 2. a state of wretchedness, 3. fat or fleshy, 4. lecture, 5. a revelation, 6. being useful to achieve a desired end, 7. to strengthen, 8. marked by great detail, 9. one primarily concerned with oneself, 10. not open or direct

LESSON 44

Practice A. 1. bilateral, 2. mortify, 3. marathon, 4. fluctuate, 5. morose, 6. remnant, 7. gratuitous, 8. binary, 9. prerequisite, 10. definitive

Practice B. 1. involving two sides, 2. relating to base two, 3. final, 4. to continually change, 5. granted without any charge, 6. endurance race, 7. sad, 8. to cause to feel shame, 9. something required beforehand, 10. remainder

LESSON 45

Practice A. 1. contrite, 2. acrid, 3. autonomous, 4. biennial, 5. automaton, 6. bilingual, 7. annuity, 8. podiatrist, 9. biopsy, 10. ameliorate

Practice B. 1. sharp, 2. to make better, 3. an investment yielding a fixed sum of money payable yearly, 4. something that acts like a machine, 5. functioning independently, 6. occurring every two years, 7. able to use two languages well, 8. the cutting out of a piece of human tissue for examination, 9. feeling remorse, 10. foot doctor

MULTIPLE-CHOICE ASSSESSMENT LESSONS 43–45

Lesson 43: (1) c, (2) c, (3) a, (4) c, (5) b, (6) b, (7) d, (8) c, (9) a, (10) d

Lesson 44: (11) b, (12) c, (13) c, (14) d, (15) d, (16) d, (17) a, (18) c, (19) b, (20) a

Lesson 45: (21) a, (22) c, (23) d, (24) b, (25) d, (26) c, (27) b, (28) b, (29) b, (30) a

LESSON 46

Practice A. 1. phobia, 2. disparity, 3. succinct, 4. exacerbate, 5. endemic, 6. accreditation, 7. microbe, 8. unison, 9. putrid, 10. purify

Practice B. 1. a vouching for, 2. difference, 3. native to a particular place, 4. to aggravate, 5. a very small living thing, 6. extreme fear, 7. to rid of pollutants, 8. foul smelling, 9. terse, 10. a saying together

LESSON 47

Practice A. 1. emigrate, 2. demagogue, 3. anarchy, 4. alias, 5. monotonous, 6. monopoly, 7. creditor, 8. speculate, 9. autocracy, 10. alienate

Practice B. 1. another name, 2. to make others unfriendly to one, 3. disorder, 4. a form of government in which one person has absolute power, 5. one to whom a sum of money is owed, 6. a person who stirs up the emotions of people to become a leader and achieve selfish ends, 7. to leave one's country for elsewhere, 8. excessive control of a product in a given market, 9. uniform, 10. to take part in any risky business venture

LESSON 48

Practice A. 1. creed, 2. nadir, 3. centipede, 4. emancipate, 5. claustrophobia, 6. credential, 7. anonymous, 8. unilateral, 9. symbiotic, 10. antipathy

Practice B. 1. lacking a name, 2. a dislike for someone, 3. a wormlike animal with many legs, 4. extreme fear of being confined in a small place, 5. a document such as a degree, 6. belief, 7. to set free, 8. the lowest point, 9. referring to mutual interdependence on one another, 10. one-sided

MULTIPLE-CHOICE ASSSESSMENT LESSONS 46–48

Lesson 46: (1) c, (2) b, (3) d, (4) a, (5) a, (6) c, (7) d, (8) c, (9) d, (10) c

Lesson 47: (11) d, (12) d, (13) a, (14) d, (15) d, (16) c, (17) c, (18) b, (19) c, (20) b

Lesson 48: (21) c, (22) c, (23) d, (24) d, (25) d, (26) c, (27) c, (28) c, (29) b, (30) b

LESSON 49

Practice A. 1. vicissitude, 2. anthropomorphic, 3. potential, 4. misogamist, 5. omnipotent, 6. omniscient, 7. genealogy, 8. polygamy, 9. omnipresent, 10. pungent

Practice B. 1. giving human shape or characteristics to gods, animals, objects, and so forth, 2. the tracing of one's ancestors, 3. hater of marriage, 4. all-powerful, 5. being present everywhere at the same time, 6. all-knowing, 7. marriage to many spouses at the same time, 8. possible ability one has, 9. biting, 10. a condition of change

LESSON 50

Practice A. 1. trauma, 2. capitulate, 3. specious, 4. pseudonym, 5. chronological, 6. collateral, 7. perception, 8. misnomer, 9. convocation, 10. synthesis

Practice B. 1. surrender, 2. arranged in time order, 3. something given as security for a mortgage to protect the lender, 4. an academic assembly, 5. a name wrongly applied, 6. the act of becoming aware of something through the senses, 7. false name, 8. faulty reasoning, 9. a putting together of two or more things, 10. an injury

LESSON 51

Practice A. 1. vestige, 2. dialect, 3. extemporaneous, 4. facsimile, 5. faction, 6. ubiquitous, 7. travesty, 8. putative, 9. infinitesimal, 10. manipulation

Practice B. 1. a variety of speech, 2. spoken without any preparation, 3. an exact copy, 4. a number of people in a group, 5. too small to be measured, 6. the act of managing skillfully, 7. commonly accepted or supposed, 8. ridiculous imitation for purposes of ridicule, 9. present or seeming to be present everywhere at the same time, 10. a trace.

MULTIPLE-CHOICE ASSSESSMENT LESSONS 49–51

Lesson 49: (1) b, (2) c, (3) a, (4) d, (5) b, (6) c, (7) b, (8) c, (9) b, (10) d

Lesson 50: (11) a, (12) b, (13) d, (14) c, (15) b, (16) b, (17) a, (18) b, (19) a, (20) c

Lesson 51: (21) c, (22) c, (23) b, (24) d, (25) a, (26) b, (27) c, (28) d, (29) a, (30) c

LESSON 52

Practice A. 1. hacker, 2. interactive, 3. browser, 4. Internet, 5. scanner, 6. cineplex, 7. cloning, 8. cybernetics, 9. e-mailed, 10. cyberspace

Practice B. 1. software that allows a user to search through information on a server, 2. a cinema complex, 3. producing an identical duplicate from a cell, 4. science dealing with complex electronic systems, 5. electronic system of interlinked networks of computers, 6. electronic mail, 7. a computer expert, 8. acting on one another, 9. computer network, 10. optical device that records information for transmission

Glossary of Words

Abridge	Lesson 24	Anthropology	Lesson 30
Absolve	Lesson 17	Anthropomorphic	Lesson 49
Abstract	Lesson 25	Anticipate	Lesson 13
Abyss	Lesson 43	Antipathy	Lesson 48
Accountability	Lesson 29	Apathy	Lesson 19
Accreditation	Lesson 46	Appraise	Lesson 10
Acquisition	Lesson 9	Apprehensive	Lesson 8
Acrid	Lesson 45	Apprise	Lesson 11
Adamant	Lesson 16	Approbation	Lesson 35
Adaptation	Lesson 2	Apt	Lesson 24
Adept	Lesson 9	Archaic	Lesson 33
Adversary	Lesson 9	Archetype	Lesson 21
Adversity	Lesson 43	Arrogant	Lesson 21
Aesthetic	Lesson 7	Assess	Lesson 18
Affinity	Lesson 27	Assessment	Lesson 29
Affirm	Lesson 3	Asset	Lesson 1
Affluent	Lesson 5	Assimilate	Lesson 42
Affront	Lesson 7	Assumption	Lesson 12
Agile	Lesson 35	Assurance	Lesson 12
Agnostic	Lesson 33	Astrology	Lesson 30
Alias	Lesson 47	Astronomy	Lesson 30
Alien	Lesson 21	Astute	Lesson 13
Alienate	Lesson 47	Atheist	Lesson 33
Allot	Lesson 1	Attitude	Lesson 7
Alternative	Lesson 5	Attrition	Lesson 24
Ameliorate	Lesson 45	Austere	Lesson 25
Ambidextrous	Lesson 36	Authentic	Lesson 29
Ambiguous	Lesson 31	Autocracy	Lesson 47
Ameliorate	Lesson 45	Automaton	Lesson 45
Amend	Lesson 24	Autonomous	Lesson 45
Amiable	Lesson 16	Avail	Lesson 16
Amnesty	Lesson 6	Aversion	Lesson 42
Amoral	Lesson 16	Avocation	Lesson 34
Anachronism	Lesson 34	Awe	Lesson 22
Anarchy	Lesson 47	Awry	Lesson 12
Anecdote	Lesson 9		
Angst	Lesson 42	Beguile	Lesson 19
Animate	Lesson 37	Bellicose	Lesson 38
Animosity	Lesson 17	Belligerent	Lesson 31
Animus	Lesson 37	Bibliophile	Lesson 40
Annuity	Lesson 45	Bibliotherapy	Lesson 40
Anonymous	Lesson 48	Biennial	Lesson 45
Antagonize	Lesson 7	Bigamy	Lesson 33
Antecedent	Lesson 2	Bilateral	Lesson 44